Environmental Capacity Enhancement Project

Environmental Roundtable Series

John Devlin, series editor

TABLE OF CONTENTS

This book is dedicated to the memory of Dr. Isaac Sindiga who passed away suddenly, shortly after this project was completed.

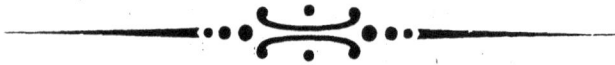

SERIES PREFACE

The Environmental Capacity Enhancement Project (ECEP) has sought over the past four years to contribute to improved regional environmental management in Eastern and Southern Africa. The project has involved participants from 13 countries (Angola, Botswana, Kenya, Lesotho, Malawi, Mozambique, Namibia, South Africa, Swaziland, Tanzania, Uganda, Zambia, Zimbabwe) and has concentrated upon six environmental areas: eco-tourism, ecological agriculture, land use planning, small scale mining, waste management and watershed management. The project has not sought to develop a narrow set of regional environmental experts. Rather it has sought to bring together development practitioners, activists, analysts, researchers and policy-makers so that all could become familiar with the policy options and technology choices available to respond to the complex range of environmental problems shared across the region.

The regional training courses, the collaborative research projects, and the professional exchanges supported by ECEP have created multistakeholder venues where representatives from governmental and non-governmental institutions, the private sector and academic institutions could build linkages for mutual support and on-going information exchange. During its four years of operation ECEP has graduated 180 from its training courses and funded 53· collaborative research projects involving 125 principal researchers. It has also supported 35 professional enhancement attachments of which 27 have involved exchanges between different countries. Having brought environmental practitioners together ECEP then sought to establish the conditions for continued networking among them so that the regional and multistakeholder perspective would be maintained over the long term. Six networks of researchers and practitioners have been created. And all have had an opportunity to meet during the networking conference held in Harare from May 13-15, 1998 to exchange papers, discuss their future organizational efforts and evaluate what had been achieved to date.

The final outputs of the project are the five volumes of collected papers comprising the Environmental Roundtable Series. These five volumes represent the best of documents and reports that have been produced by ECEP participants. They will serve not only as valuable collections for environmental policy makers, environmental educators and environmental activists but also as catalysts for future initiatives dedicated to building an effective environmental management culture in the region. The preparation of this series has been made possible by two important groups. First, the Canadian International Development Agency, which has generously funded ECEP over the past four years. Second, the many ECEP participants who have generously donated their time and energy to making this project a success. Their contributions are acknowledged with thanks.

Dr. R.J. McLaughlin
Dean, Ontario Agricultural College, University of Guelph, Canada
March 1999

PREFACE

Ecotourism is on the minds of many governments and institutions engaged in development throughout the world. Unfortunately, its implementation has not always produced the expected results. When done right, ecotourism has provided income to local people while minimizing the impact on the natural and social environment. However, when the direction of tourism is influenced by governments' need to earn massive amounts of foreign currency and create jobs, ecotourism has become as destructive as the alternative uses of the natural resource base it was designed to replace. Many more of the intricacies of the implementation of ecotourism need to be understood if the first outcome is to prevail over the latter. For this reason, the Environmental Capacity Enhancement Project (ECEP) included ecotourism in its repertoire of subjects to be investigated.

This book is a collection of chapters based on research that resulted from the ecotourism section of the ECEP project. Contributing authors completed ecotourism research projects in Eastern or Southern Africa during the three years of ECEP, from 1995 to 1998. The subject of the book is ecotourism, a specific type of tourism that focuses on conservation of the environment while creating benefits for local populations and communities. A further definition will be provided in the chapters which follow, but it is important to point out that the contributing authors made central the concept of community in their definitions of ecotourism.

Each chapter takes a holistic perspective on the subject, in that it connects tourism to environment conservation and community development. All the chapters assume that by making local communities central in decision-making, environmental preservation will become a priority for people as they, and their communities, experience benefits through tourism activity.

The intention of the volume is not only to discuss the results of the research conducted under the sponsorship of ECEP, but to also provide a methodological guide for those contemplating future research projects in ecotourism in Sub-Saharan Africa. The chapters contained in this text are different in that respect. Each chapter provides a short description of the methodology through which the research was conducted. The reader will be able to assess the methodology in juxtaposition to the goals, objectives and the outcomes of each of the research projects reported here. In that sense, the text is meant to be instructive.

The chapters are similar in format but different in content. The first two chapters set the stage for the book. In chapter one, Isaac Sindiga presents an overview of tourism development in Africa. Chapter two follows that introduction with a brief discussion of the concept and definition of ecotourism. Chapters three through eight present case studies based on research. The last chapter is unique in that it discusses a project which is ongoing in the western part of the Cape in South Africa. This chapter does not focus on tourism research *per se,* but demonstrates how an archeology research project can be utilized as an ecotourism destination in order to protect the archeology, environment and culture of the area.

This volume would not have been possible without the support and active participation of many individuals. Special appreciation is offered to John Gaudi and Scott McConnell, editorial assistants, for their detailed examination of the draft manuscripts as the chapters progressed. Kathy MacLean of the ECEP office at the University of Guelph was also very helpful in the development of this volume. Stephanie Wells, copy editor, and Irene Staunton, who coordinated the publication of this book in Zimbabwe, are thanked for the expertise they provided. A special thank-you is rendered to the contributing authors for their patience in the editing process.

Donald G. Reid

CONTRIBUTORS

Valerie Baron
   M.Sc. Student (since completed)
   Department of Rural Extension Studies, University of Guelph
   Guelph, Canada

Nina Cohen
   Cohen & Judin
   Cape Town, South Africa

Nadine Evans
   M.Sc. Student, School of Rural Planning and Development
   University of Guelph
   Guelph, Canada

Excellent Hachileka
   Lecturer, Department of Geography
   University of Zambia
   Lusaka, Zambia

Hilton Judin
   Cohen & Judin
   Cape Town, South Africa

Reid Kreutzwiser
   Professor, Department of Geography
   University of Guelph
   Guelph, Canada

Mary Leslie
   Department of Archaeology
   University of Cape Town
   Cape Town, South Africa

Lois Lindsay
   M.A. Student, Department of Geography
   University of Guelph
   Guelph, Canada

Alicia Monis
   Department of Arts, Culture, Science and Technology
   Pretoria, South Africa

Rushdi Nackerdien
   Independant Electoral Commission (IEC)
   Pretoria, South Africa
Ray Naguran
   Lecturer, Department of Economics
   University of Durban-Westville
   Durban, South Africa
Dan Nuttall
   Ph.D. Student, School of Landscape Architecture
   University of Guelph
   Guelph, Canada
Stephen Ongaro
   Lecturer, Department of Tourism
   Moi University
   Eldoret, Kenya
John Parkington
   Professor, Department of Archaeology
   University of Western Cape
   Cape Town, South Africa
Juanita Pastor
   Robben Island Museum
   Robben Island, South Africa
Colette Peitersen
   Department of Archaeology
   University of Cape Town
   Cape Town, South Africa
Sandra Prosalendis
   District Six Museum Foundation
   Cape Town, South Africa
Donald G. Reid
   Professor, School of Rural Planning and Development
   University of Guelph
   Guelph, Canada

Jenny Sandler
  Cohen & Judin
  Cape Town, South Africa
Isaac Sindiga (deceased)
  Principal, Kisii College Campus
  Egerton University
  Kisii, Kenya
Vincent Taylor
  Senior Lecturer, School of Environmental Studies
  University of Western Cape
  Cape Town, South Africa

Chapter 1

TOURISM IN SUB-SAHARAN AFRICA

by Isaac Sindiga

INTRODUCTION

This chapter examines the patterns of tourism development in Sub-Saharan Africa with special reference to regional cooperation and intra-Africa tourism activity[1]. It also discusses the viability of tourism as a development strategy for the continent, using a number of performance indicators, namely, foreign exchange receipts, employment, government revenues, and regional development.

Tourism's potential contribution to development has become especially important because of Sub-Saharan Africa's declining economic performance. Many African countries initially tried to develop economically by expanding and increasing the range of primary exports from agriculture and mining. When this did not provide satisfactory results, Africa turned to industrialization as a road to quick and sustainable economic growth. Contemporary Africa's endemic economic stagnation and poverty suggest that these strategies have not worked for the continent. It is in this context that attention has focused on tourism's contribution to development (de Kadt, 1976; Gamble, 1989; Summary, 1987).

This inquiry into the role of tourism in development is not intended to narrow the discussion to tourism's economic contribution to Sub-Saharan Africa. This is the fashion of most assessments — to touch only on the macro-economic characteristics — in a word, the business of tourism. Such studies focus on the transnational companies operating the tourism business and the national governments which invite them. Seldom are questions asked about how tourism affects social structures or contributes to development at the local level. Development is not merely a rise in the per capita incomes. It subsumes "reduction of poverty and greater equity to progress in education, health and nutrition, and to the *protection of the environment*" (World Bank, 1991, p. 4). Only environmental protection through effective resource management strategies can assure sustainable development.

1

Tourism in the context of African development must contribute towards poverty alleviation and the continent's overall economic progress. Perhaps a mix of strategies, including agricultural transformation, industrialization, and tourism development, is required to mobilize Sub-Saharan Africa's production forces by making optimal use of the existing natural resources. Carefully planned tourism development could provide crucial resources for African economic transformation – in tune with the aspirations of the peoples of the continent.

More than two decades ago, Elkan urged that any assessment of the role of tourism should be eclectic and that each country case should be considered separately because "the balance of advantage is greatly dependent upon the policies pursued with regard to the particular form of hotel and tourist development" (1975, p. 123). Yet lessons from tourism development elsewhere in the world can be brought to bear on a particular case in order to see the common threads which run through them.

PATTERNS OF GLOBAL TOURISM

Tourism and travel are the world's largest industry in terms of the numbers of people participating, the amount of resources generated, and employment capacity. International tourist arrivals have been increasing steadily from 362 million people in 1987 to 458 million in 1990 to 518 million in 1993 and 594 million in 1996 (Table 1.1).

Table 1.1 Arrivals of tourists from abroad and percentage share by region (thousands)*

Regions	1987	1988	1989	1990	1991	1992	1993	1994	1995	1996	Ave Share
World	362,295	395,024	426,636	458,331	463,647	503,148	517,973	544,524	564,025	593,745	
Percent share	100.00	100.00	100.00	100.00	100.00	100.00	100.00	100.00	100.00	100.00	
Africa	9,833	12,508	13,822	15,058	16,202	17,841	18,327	18,652	19,211	20,091	
Percent share	2.7	3.16	3.24	3.3	3.49	3.55	3.54	3.4	3.4	3.38	3.3%
Americas	74,901	83,078	86,862	93,394	96,492	103,412	103,703	106,433	110,766	115,517	
Percent share	20.67	21.03	20.36	20.40	20.80	20.55	20.02	19.54	19.64	19.45	20.2%
East Asia/Pacific	39,361	45,755	46,419	53,220	54,987	62,749	69,581	75,170	79,658	86,792	
Percent share	10.86	11.58	10.88	11.60	11.86	12.47	13.43	13.86	14.12	14.6	12.5%
Europe	228,791	842,467	267,910	284,521	284,320	305,062	311,949	328,224	336,378	351,612	
Percent share	63.15	61.38	62.80	62.05	61.32	60.63	60.22	60.3	59.64	59.22	61%
Middle East	6,702	8,335	8,569	8,959	8,366	10,475	10,854	12,099	13,711	15,256	
Percent share	1.85	2.1	2.0	1.95	1.8	2.08	2.09	2.22	2.43	2.57	2.1%
South Asia	2,707	2,881	3,054	3,179	3,280	3,609	3,559	3,946	4,301	4,471	
Percent share	0.75	0.73	0.72	0.69	0.70	0.72	0.69	0.72	0.76	0.75	0.7%

Source: World Tourism Organisation (WTO), Personal communication, April 2, 1997.

*Note: The percentage figures may not add up to 100.00 because of rounding.

If the present rate of growth continues at 4 percent per year, the World Tourism Organization (WTO) projects that global tourism will reach 700 million international arrivals by 2000 and 937 million by 2010. Similarly, the resources generated by tourism are growing impressively. In the mid-1990s, tourism accounted for more than 10 percent of the world total gross domestic product. International tourism receipts (excluding international transport) increased from US$175,000 million in 1987 to US$266,000 million in 1990 and US$425,000 million in 1996 (Table 1.2). It is projected that receipts from tourism will increase to US$600,000 million by the year 2000. In terms of global capital investments in infrastructure, facilities and equipment, and employment generation, tourism is a giant industry. One estimate indicates that one out of sixteen people in the world works in tourism (Richter, 1992). Without considering the quality of that employment, this figure points to tourism's major significance in the global economy.

The geographical patterns of world tourism show great differences in international arrivals and receipts. Europe, North America and Japan generate the greatest numbers of tourists. Table 1.1 shows international tourist arrivals from abroad by region and year using the classification of the WTO. For the 10-year period represented by these data, Europe received 61 percent of the arrivals, followed by the Americas (20.2 percent), East Asia/Pacific (12.5 percent), Africa (3.3 percent), the Middle East (2.1 percent) and South Asia with 0.7 percent. The tourism receipts appear to follow a similar pattern (Table 1.2).

Table 1.2 International tourism receipts (excluding international transport) and percentage share by region (US$ million)

Region/sub-region	1987	1988	1989	1990	1991	1992	1993	1994	1995	1996	Ave share
World	174,609	202,556	219,477	266,207	272,684	310,785	317,790	351,179	398,898	425,047	
Africa	3,787	4,567	4,508	5,333	5,009	6,023	6,133	6,511	6,980	7,670	
% share	2.2	2.3	2.1	2.00	1.8	1.9	1.9	1.9	1.8	1.8	2.0
Americas	42,873	51,374	60,238	70,201	77,683	85,524	91,151	95,109	100,225	106,308	
% share	24.6	25.4	27.5	26.4	28.5	27.5	28.7	27.1	25.13	25.0	26.6
East Asia/Pacific	22,671	30,397	34,142	38,841	40,203	47,278	52,411	62,198	73,411	82.156	
% share	13.0	15.00	15.6	14.6	14.7	15.2	16.5	17.7	18.4	19.3	16.0
Europe	98,098	109,225	113,128	144,602	143,098	163,722	160,470	178,751	207,351	216,913	
% share	56.2	53.9	51.5	54.3	52.5	52.7	50.5	50.9	52.0	51.0	52.6
Middle East	5,305	5,090	5,434	5,147	4,280	5,400	4,832	5,437	7,285	8,037	
% share	3.0	2.5	2.5	1.9	1.6	1.7	1.5	1.6	1.8	1.9	2.0
South Asia	1,875	1,903	2,027	2,083	2,411	2,838	2,793	3,178	3,646	3,963	
% share	1.1	0.9	0.9	0.8	0.9	0.9	0.9	0.9	0.9	0.9	0.9

Source: WTO. Personal communication, 2 April 1997.

These aggregate figures provide the macro picture of tourism patterns at the global scale. They do, however, conceal the relatively large differences within any one region. There are large variations in these differences and some countries are better endowed than others in tourism activity. Also, there is substantial domestic tourism activity within individual countries, especially in the developed world. The data for such internal travel which generates much revenue and employment are not reflected in this discussion.

PATTERNS OF TOURISM IN AFRICA

Africa's share of the world tourism market appears rather small for the geographical size of the continent and its population. International tourist arrivals increased from about 10 million in 1987 to 15 million in 1990, 18 million in 1993 and 20 million in 1996 (Table 1.3).

Table 1.3 Arrivals of tourists from abroad to Africa (thousands)*

Region	1987	1988	1989	1990	1991	1992	1993	1994	1995	1996
World	362,295	395,024	426,636	458,331	463,647	503,148	517,973	544,524	564,025	593,745
Africa	9,833	12,508	13,822	15,058	16,202	17,841	18,327	18,652	19,211	20,091
Eastern Africa[1]	2,132	2,335	2,460	2,852	2,944	3,069	3,459	3,706	4,134	4,810
Middle Africa[2]	247	264	345	350	356	320	304	287	335	332
North Africa[3]	4,953	7,313	7,920	8,398	8,595	9,067	8,826	8,138	7,252	7,193
South Africa[4]	1,331	1,379	1,795	2,006	2,961	3,945	4,357	5,053	5,932	6,118
Western Africa[5]	1,170	1,217	1,302	1,452	1,346	1,440	1,381	1,468	1,558	1,638

[1]Eastern Africa: Burundi, Comoros, Djibouti, Ethiopia, Kenya, Madagascar, Malawi, Mauritius, Reunion, Rwanda, Seychelles, Somalia, Tanzania, Uganda, Zambia and Zimbabwe
[2]Middle Africa: Angola, Cameroon, Central African Republic, Chad, Congo, Gabon, Sao Tome and Principe, and Zaire
[3]North Africa: Algeria, Morocco, Sudan, Tunisia (the WTO counts Egypt and Libya in Middle East)
[4]Southern Africa: Botswana, Lesotho, Namibia, South Africa and Swaziland
[5]Western Africa: Benin, Burkina Faso, Cape Verde, Cote d'Ivoire, The Gambia, Ghana, Guinea, Mali, Niger, Nigeria, Senegal, Sierra Leone and Togo

Source: WTO, Personal communication, 2 April 1997.

International tourism receipts (excluding international transport) increased from US$3800 million in 1987 to $5300 million in 1990, $6100 million in 1993 and $7700 million in 1996 (Table 1.4).

Table 1.4 International tourism receipts
(excluding international transport) (US$ Million)

Region/Subregion	1987	1988	1989	1990	1991	1992	1993	1994	1995	1996
World	174,609	202,552	219,477	266,207	272,684	310,785	317,790	351,179	398,898	425,047
Africa	3,787	4,567	4,508	5,333	5,009	6,023	6,133	6,511	6,980	7,670
Eastern Africa	854	797	898	1,116	1,070	1,251	1,266	1,404	1,639	1,888
Middle Africa	71	67	125	102	109	106	116	122	116	118
North Africa	17,22	2,458	2,188	2,297	1,829	2.514	2,418	2,622	2,521	2,751
South Africa	669	745	801	1,243	1,409	1,515	1,694	1,816	2,073	2,238
Western Africa	471	500	496	575	592	637	639	547	631	675

Source: WTO. Personal communication. 2 April 1997.

When these figures are viewed within the perspective of world tourism in general, they are comparatively low. The arrivals as a proportion of the world total made up only 2.5 percent in 1980; 2.9 percent in 1985; 3.3 percent in 1990; 3.5 percent in 1993; and 3.4 percent in 1996 (see Table 1.1, Dieke, 1995). However, receipts from international tourism declined from 2.5 percent in 1980 to 2.2 percent in 1985 to 2 percent in 1990; 1.9 percent in 1993; and 1.8 percent in 1996 (see Table 1.4, Dieke, 1995). These figures indicate that the absolute numbers of tourist arrivals are not necessarily reflected in foreign exchange earnings. Perhaps many of the visitors to Africa spend little money for reasons which are discussed later in this chapter. Overall, these figures show that Africa as a region for world tourism is rather poorly developed.

Within Africa, there is great variation in terms of the numbers of tourist arrivals and foreign exchange earnings (see Tables 1.3 and 1.4). Most tourists go to North Africa, South Africa and Eastern Africa. For example, of the 20 million tourist arrivals from abroad in 1996, about 36 percent went to North Africa[2], 30.5 percent to South Africa[3], 23.9 percent to Eastern Africa, 8.15 percent to Western Africa and 1.6 percent to Middle Africa. The receipts from tourism reflect a similar ranking in magnitude (see Table 1.4). Indeed, over the continent tourism appears to be well developed only in a few countries. These are Tunisia; South Africa; Morocco; Zimbabwe; Kenya; Botswana; Mauritius; and Namibia (Table 1.5).

Table 1.5 Leading tourism destinations in Africa by international arrivals, 1996

	Arrivals (Thousands)	Receipts US$ million
South Africa	4640	1738
Tunisia	3885	1436
Morocco	2693	1292
Zimbabwe	1743	219
Kenya	907	493
Botswana	660	178
Mauritius	435	473
Namibia	405	265
Reunion	339	-
Tanzania	326	322

Source: WTO, Personal communication, 2 April 1997.

In general, there are relatively fewer tourists in West Africa where the major attractions are the cultural heritage of the area, especially for African-Americans, and medieval empires (Williams, 1976). The spectacular scenery such as the East African Rift Valley system, volcanic mountains and national parks are missing in West Africa.

This rather poor picture of tourism in Sub-Saharan Africa might be turned around by regional cooperation to encourage the easy movement of tourists across common borders and to establish joint packages for multi-destination travellers. This could increase the global competitiveness of African tourism. This is feasible, given that Africa already has more than 200 regional cooperation organizations, of which 160 are intergovernmental and the rest are non-governmental (World Bank, 1989, p. 149).

REGIONAL COOPERATION IN AFRICAN TOURISM DEVELOPMENT

Regional cooperation has been suggested as a viable way of obtaining the greatest benefits from African tourism through increasing its competitiveness. The clearest statement on this matter was put forward by African leaders in the 1980 Lagos Plan of Action (LPA) (World Bank, 1989; Dieke, 1995). LPA suggested the current structure, organization and management of African tourism – which emphasizes foreign ownership and management of tourist enterprises – should be reversed. LPA espoused the view that tourism on the continent should be promoted, controlled and managed by the Africans themselves, and not dominated by western multinational companies as it is today.

Specifically, the LPA put forward the following goals for African tourism: development of intra-African tourism; provide technical training for African staff in order to gain competence to manage tourism enterprises; create interstate or intra-regional tourist circuits; and develop regional cooperation so as to utilize Africa's varied tourism resources in an efficient manner (Dieke, 1995, p. 88).

The idea of regional cooperation in tourism is part of wider thinking on pooling Africa's vast but largely fragmented resources to reverse the continent's economic decline and put it back on the road to development. This approach emphasizes Africa's self-reliance through the promotion of regional groupings of states and by encouraging trade and economic development within the region (World Bank, 1989; Nyong'o, 1990; Courier, 1988; UNECA, 1989). It identifies one of Africa's development problems to be small economies which characteristically have low levels of income and small population sizes. Ndiaye (1990, p. 36) has argued that:

The problem of small economies is a widespread phenomenon in the continent. Today some thirty countries accounting for about one-half of independent Africa's total population have income per head of less than 350 United States dollars per year. Only seven countries, with less than 10 percent of Africa's population have income per capita of 1,000 US dollars or more.

About half of Africa's countries have a population of less than five million each; 13 countries have an area of less than 50,000 sq. km. each while 13 are landlocked (UNECA, 1989, p. 5). Within individual countries, particularly geographically large countries, population centres are unevenly distributed, making it difficult to develop transport networks and supply basic services such as water and electricity. This is partly inherited from the colonial period when transport was often created for the outward expropriation of resources rather than to serve indigenous populations.

The rather low personal incomes add to the small size of the markets, making it difficult for single countries to support modern enterprises. Tourism is one of the sectors which can benefit from market integration and increased cooperation within Africa. Indeed, regionalism is seen to be one of the critical considerations of tourism development in Africa; the other is multiple destination marketing (Teye, 1991, p. 288).

Regional development of tourism in Africa is supported by a number of arguments. The continent offers a great diversity of attractions ranging from historical and archaeological monuments to physical landscapes, cultural pluralism and very rich flora and fauna. However, the tourism industry, as currently established, yields inequitable benefits to the disadvantage of Africa. If Africa's tourism initiatives were united, different countries would be able to pool their attractions and cooperate in terms of capital, infrastructure and human resources to serve the needs of tourism (Teye, 1991; Dieke, 1995). Further, removing administrative obstacles which make tourism costly to the tourists could increase tourist flows (Mitchell, 1970, p.13).

Tourism activities can benefit by substantial economies of scale when planned on a regional basis (Mitchell, 1970, p. 12; Popovic, 1972, p. 50). Joint infrastructure development, planning, marketing research, and training could be done at less cost, to the advantage of the cooperating member countries. Regional efforts could also give Africa better leverage in dealing with large tourism institutions in the west (Dieke, 1995; Teye, 1991).

Regional cooperation could also reduce competition for tourists between neighbouring states and enhance gains from the tourism industry. In terms of promotion, it is more effective to market a region with its varied tourism resources than a single country (Popovic, 1972).

Joint promotion does not mean that the unique features of individual countries would not be highlighted. Rather, each country would be promoted as part of a region with many things to see, giving the tourist a choice of visiting one country or several countries within the region. Visitors from western Europe, North America and the Far East want to see as much as possible because the journey to Sub-Saharan Africa is long and expensive. This provides further rationale for regional cooperation and marketing.

Regional cooperation could also start to overcome the prevailing negative perceptions about the continent and provide meaning to an African identity. This identity goes beyond policy actions, infrastructure development and the creation of institutions to "a more fundamental need to mobilize the media and educational and cultural institutions to promote the concept that cooperation within Africa is likely to enhance the progress of all African societies" (World Bank, 1989, p. 161). This approach calls for changes in attitudes among Africans and the engendering of small-scale cooperative relationships among people of different countries.

A systematic program to achieve this could include organizing seminars, workshops, and exchange visits for African journalists; establishing a regional information center to produce and distribute feature articles, pamphlets, videos, and films; and incorporating courses on African history, culture, and economics into school curriculums, especially at the University and postgraduate levels [sic]. In addition relaxing travel restrictions and residence requirements would encourage increased contacts within Africa at the personal level (ibid., 1989, p. 161).

Multiple destination marketing is probably viable through regional cooperation because it allows possibilities for diversifying the tourism product (Teye, 1991) and offering the visitor a wide variety of attractions in one trip. Multi-destination tourism is recognized as an important component of travel among Southern African countries. The promotion of regional and international cooperation in tourism is a policy objective of the Namibian government (Namibia, n.d., p. 228). Until the mid-1970s, tourism in East Africa was sold as a single package and a visitor could travel in Kenya, Uganda and Tanzania in one trip. Such an arrangement was possible under the auspices of the East African Community (EAC). The 1977 break-up of the EAC forced each country to market its tourist attractions independently. The result was less competitive packages for international visitors to East Africa.

INTRA-AFRICA TOURISM

Africa depends on tourists from the developed countries rather than on intra-regional and domestic sources (Dieke, 1995; Teye, 1991). Table 1.6 shows the origins of the tourist arrivals in Africa as recorded in 1995. However, tourism statistics in Africa must be read with caution. There is no accurate information, especially on intra-Africa tourism.

Table 1.6 Tourist origins to Africa, 1995

Destination	Total arrivals (Thousands)	Africa (Percent)	Outside Africa (Percent)
Africa	19045	46.2	53.8
Eastern Africa	3968	46.4	53.6
Middle Africa	335	10.0	90.0
North Africa	7252	16.0	84.0
Southern Africa	5932	84.7	15.3
Western Africa	1558	46.9	53.1

Source: WTO, Personal communication, 28 February 1997.

Intra-Africa tourism largely remains an informal activity; it goes on across the borders but remains either poorly recorded or unrecorded, just like other informal economic activities on the continent (Ellis and MacGaffey, 1996). With this caveat in mind, it appears from Table 1.6 that only 46.2 percent of the tourist arrivals in African countries came from within Africa, and the majority came from outside the continent.

But the data are highly variable according to sub-region and require further explanation. While North Africa received most of its tourists from other regions of the world, Southern Africa recorded huge intra-Africa tourism flows accounting for 84.7 percent of the total. There is much intra-regional movement in Southern Africa, especially the Republic of South Africa and Botswana. This is probably a result of South Africa's enormous economic strength. Many people move into South Africa from neighbouring countries to work a few months in the mines and docks and then return home. Others probably visit South Africa for business purposes. In 1993, 60.8 percent of the tourist arrivals in Namibia were from South Africa; intra-Africa tourism accounted for 77 percent of the arrivals (Namibia, n.d., p. 226). Overall, visitor and tour operator surveys indicate that visitors to Namibia combine trips to South Africa, Zimbabwe and Botswana (Namibia, n.d., p. 225) showing the importance of multi-destination tourism.

Table 1.7 Tourist origins for selected African countries, 1995

	Total arrivals (thousands)	Receipts (US$ million)	Origin	
			Africa (Percent)	Outside Africa (Percent)
Kenya	691	454	26.5	73.5
Uganda	189	79	-	-
Tanzania	295	259	39.0	61.0
Zimbabwe	1,363	154	85.4	14.6
Mauritius	422	430	340	66.0
Botswana	644	162	-	-
Namibia	399	263	-	-
Ghana	286	233	34.0	66.0
Senegal	280	130	20.2	79.8
Cote d'Ivoire	188	72	55.7	44.3
Swaziland	300	35	84.5	15.5

Source: WTO. Personal communication, 28 February 1997.

Table 1.7 shows a somewhat detailed picture of the origins of tourists in selected African countries in 1995. Except for Zimbabwe and Swaziland, the other countries are heavily dependent on visitors from outside the continent. Many of the tourists into Zimbabwe and Swaziland are South Africans who visit over weekends or for a few days and generally spend little money. Although Zimbabwe recorded the largest number of arrivals, its tourism receipts are only modest, suggesting that intra-Africa tourists generally spend little. This is also the case with Swaziland. Perhaps for this reason, many countries tend to market their tourism to the western countries. This is not merely an effort to earn foreign exchange required for investment and development purposes; it is also because holiday tourism is a product of western affluence, materialism, and lifestyle. A number of authors have noted that pleasure tourism tends to be limited in Africa (Teye, 1991; Dieke, 1995). Dieke (1995, p. 76) has summarized the situation as follows:

> ...indigenous African's demand for travel is penalized by their low income per capita and extended family commitments and therefore their modest purchasing power. In this sense, it is not leisure but visiting-friends-and-relatives (VFR) tourism – mainly for family reasons – that predominates in much of Africa. Even the African elites who have the means to engage in tourist activities generally tend to vacation outside Africa or to retain vertical allegiances with erstwhile European mother countries.

This probably explains the rather poor development of tourism in much of Sub-Saharan Africa.

TOURISM AND DEVELOPMENT IN AFRICA

The case for tourism and development is somewhat different from other sectors of the economy. Because it does not produce goods and services, tourism's contribution to development is indirect through generating revenues (Green, 1979, pp. 81-82). It involves the creation of an infrastructure of attractions, accommodation facilities, travel and transport, and communications which allow visitors to go to the source of an attraction. Those who think in economic terms and look at tourism as an "export" industry will say that there is no actual transference of goods. The consumer of the export must go to its source, thereby requiring that certain arrangements be made. Such preparations include packaging the tourism product, accommodation, travel and local transportation. Because of the investment demands of tourism, the industry is well developed in only a few countries including Egypt, Tunisia and Morocco in North Africa; The Gambia in

West Africa; Kenya, Mauritius and Seychelles in Eastern Africa; Zimbabwe in Central Africa; and Botswana and South Africa. For most of Africa, however, tourism development has elicited much critical commentary.

> Tourism in most sub-Sahara African countries is hardly an industry since the tourism infrastructure is weak, tourism organization is poor, and net revenue is meagre. Almost all tourist arrivals consist of African nationals, resident abroad, returning to visit friends and relatives, business visitors, and those visiting expatriate residents. The primary vacation or leisure tourism sector is undeveloped (Teye, 1991, p. 288).

So uneven is the development of international tourism activity on the continent that most of the tourism revenue goes to North Africa (see Table 1.3). In 1992, North African countries took 52 percent of the arrivals and 43 percent of the receipts followed by Southern and Eastern Africa (Dieke, 1995). Provisional data on tourism receipts, excluding international travel, for 1996 for Africa was US$1,621 million. Of this, North Africa received 35.8 percent with Southern Africa taking 29.4 percent and Eastern Africa, 24.4 percent (see Table 1.3). North Africa's predominance is probably explained by its proximity to western Europe where most of the tourists originate. Europeans, especially from Spain, France and Italy, tend to see North Africa as part of the European frontier.

Tourism is sensitive to the tastes, likes and dislikes, and personal whims of the people undertaking a trip. Sometimes meeting the expected standards for international tourism can be a daunting task. Although Nigeria, for example, traditionally has not given much priority to tourism (Lea, 1981, p. 30), leading Nigerian novelist Chinua Achebe (1984) adjudges that the country does not meet the requirements of international tourism.

> Nigeria is one of the most disorderly nations in the world. It is one of the most corrupt, insensitive, inefficient places under the sun. It is one of the most expensive countries and one of those that give least value for money. It is dirty, callous, noisy, ostentatious, dishonest and vulgar (ibid., p.10).

Despite his angry tone, Achebe emphasizes a number of elements which may discourage tourism – reputation of a destination, attitudes and behaviour of the hosts, the pricing of the tourism product, and political stability. Speaking directly to the problem of developing a vibrant tourism industry in Nigeria, Achebe complains that:

It is a measure of our self-delusion that we can talk about developing tourism in Nigeria. Only a masochist with an exuberant taste for self-violence will pick Nigeria for a holiday; only a character — seeking to know punishment and poverty at first hand! No, Nigeria may be a paradise for adventurers and pirates but not tourists (ibid., p. 10).

It is a well appreciated fact that tourists are highly sensitive to political instability which could threaten their personal safety and security (Sharpley, Sharpley and Adams, 1996; Teye, 1991). So, apart from developing the physical tourism infrastructure, political stability must be cultivated as an important factor in attracting tourism. Also in the very near future, the issue of human rights and internal governance of countries which seek to attract tourists, especially from the west, will come under scrutiny. Already, politically-motivated travel advice from western governments appears to have a profound effect on would-be tourists, with many cancelling their planned trips (see for example, Sharpley, Sharpley and Adams, 1996). Only countries which practice democratic ideals, adhere to the rule of law, and respect human rights will maintain political stability essential for tourism development.

Africa is in turmoil. The African continent of the 1990s is replete with examples of political violence from Somalia, Ethiopia, Eritrea and Sudan in the east to Rwanda, Burundi, Democratic Republic of Congo, Uganda and Chad in the centre to Angola in the south to Liberia, Sierra Leone, Guinea and Senegal in the west to western Sahara and Algeria in the north. Africa's continuing poor performance in tourist arrivals is blamed on safety fears. This may affect South Africa and most of North Africa save perhaps for Morocco. There is more to attracting tourism than merely investing in the infrastructure.

The argument for tourism as a development strategy is primarily economic, although esoteric ideals such as bringing increased understanding among peoples and cultures are invoked. Among the economic factors for developing tourism are generating foreign exchange, employment and government revenues through taxes. Tourism also aids in regional development. Each of these is considered below.

Foreign exchange

Tourism may appear to bring a large amount of hard currency into a country. Most assessments use gross foreign exchange earnings as a basis for their conclusions (de Kadt, 1976; Elkan, 1975). But this is only half the picture, as the net tourism receipts may be relatively small, and tourism has many hidden costs.

A more meaningful measure of foreign exchange receipts discounts the leakages from the gross receipts and arrives at a figure of net receipts from tourism. Many tourism enterprises in the Third World are owned and managed by western transnational companies. These companies, which monopolize the organization of international mass tourism (Brohman, 1996, p. 54), earn handsome profits by charging management fees, making limited direct investment, and through various licensing, franchise and service agreements (Lea, 1993). This keeps the parent company in a controlling position which allows it to repatriate most of the foreign exchange.

The leakages from gross tourism receipts include money used in tourism promotion through advertising and maintaining overseas offices, international air travel and local transport, interest payments, profits and remittances of wages abroad by expatriate staff. In addition, part of the foreign exchange must pay for direct purchases of food and drink from overseas, construction and maintenance of hotels, restaurants, roads and communications. A large proportion of foreign exchange reserves may be lost due to massive investments in infrastructure (Curry, 1982; Lea, 1981). The construction of an airport, for example, can consume investible surplus from tourism and other governmental resources, thereby minimizing the value of tourism to a country. Also, vehicles and spare parts are usually imported. It may be noted, however, that the quantity of imports such as food and drink will vary from one country to another. Whereas West African countries may import most of the food for tourists, this is not the case in East Africa. Here, 80 to 90 percent of the food is locally procured (Green, 1979). Even within East Africa, there are internal country differences. In Tanzania most of the food is imported, whereas Kenya produces all the food consumed by tourists in the country (Elkan, 1975, p. 129). If less food is imported, there is less foreign exchange used on this count.

Relatively large amounts of foreign exchange are lost to the developed world because of the structural dependency created through widespread foreign ownership, control and management of Third World tourism enterprises. The magnitude of the leakage varies from country to country. Estimates are thus highly variable and range from 20 to 80 percent (Lea, 1981, p. 28).

These large outflows put into question the profitability of tourism to a country. It has been argued that small, less diversified economies suffer the greatest leakages and therefore obtain the least benefits from tourism (Green, 1979;

Gamble, 1989). This reduces tourism's potential for generating broad-based development through economic growth (Brohman, 1996). In contrast, a country with a large diversified economy will reduce the imports and retain most of the foreign exchange. Kenya is frequently cited as one such example (Dieke, 1995)[4].

Contrary to the impression created in the literature, net tourism receipts or net foreign exchange earnings of tourism do not measure the net impact of tourism on gross national product.

> *Supplying tourist goods and services also requires the use of domestic resources.*
> *These resources – labour, capital, skills, land – could produce other things of value*
> *if they were not used in tourism (Mitchell, 1970, p. 2).*

The value of these "domestic" inputs must be discounted from tourism's net foreign exchange earnings before a measure of the "net tourism impact on (marginal contribution to) GNP" (*ibid.*, p. 2) can be established. This imbroglio shows the difficulty of measuring costs and benefits of tourism to the economy, leading some scholars to remark that benefits are often exaggerated (Lea, 1981, p. 25).

A further caveat can be made regarding generalizations about net foreign exchange earnings from tourism. Elkan (1975) has cautioned about applying generalizations of costs and benefits of tourism from one country's context to another. His plea is for separate assessment for individual cases because the balance of advantage depends largely on the policies which a country pursues and whether it goes for large or small-sized hotel projects. Elkan gives the example of Tanzania's development of beach hotels some distance from Dar es Salaam as a way of minimizing the socio-cultural impact of tourists on a socialist citizenry[5]. In this case, locations closer to the capital would have been more economical and could allow tourists time in Dar es Salaam in the evenings, where they would spend additional money. Elkin (1975, p. 129) persuasively concludes that policies chosen to promote tourism will have a strong bearing on its costs and benefits.

Employment

Tourism is labour-intensive. People work in the various sub-sectors of the industry, including tour-guiding, nature and cultural interpretation, game viewing, travel and transport services, promotion, sport, and in the areas of food, beverage and alcohol service and accommodation. Other tourism-related employment is in entertainment, the arts and hand-crafted curios. Indirectly, tourism creates employment in agriculture to produce food for the visitors. Infrastructure development such as road and hotel construction may provide many short-term jobs. Tourism supports other areas such as money and banking. It may also be mentioned that tourism attracts a number of activities in the informal sector. These include male and female prostitution, hawking of various merchandise, professional friendships, begging or simply following the tourists. There is also the issue of tourism and child prostitution in such countries as Sri Lanka, Thailand and the Philippines; in Africa it is reported to be on the increase in Kenya (Christian Aid, 1995). These linkages through employment tend to spread the income of tourism in a local area.

A number of estimates have been put forward on the level of employment created per hotel bed (Table 1.8).

Table 1.8 Estimates of jobs per hotel bed.

Country/Region	Jobs per bed (Direct employment)	Source
Tunisia	0.88 - 1.12	Poirier and Wright (1993:158)
North Africa	2 - 3	Green, 1979, p.84
East Africa	2 - 3	Green, 1979, p.84
Tanzania	0.80	Elkan, 1975, p.125
Kenya	0.84	Elkan, 1975, p.125

Although these data are for different years and are not strictly comparable, they do provide some indication as to the level of employment. In a strict sense, however, not all tourism requires hotel beds. Some tourists prefer outdoor camping using simple sleeping bags, but their number may be small. The hotel bed-employment ratio makes sense when considering the upmarket and mass tourism and is easily applied in many different contexts.

It has been argued that tourism creates greater employment than other forms of investment such as manufacturing (Elkan, 1975). This is used as a justification for enormous investment in tourism. But many scholars have recognized (Gamble, 1989; Elkan, 1975; Green, 1979; Lea, 1981) that it is generally more expensive to create a job in a hotel than in manufacturing. Tourism has a relatively "high ratio of capital to labour" (Green, 1979, p. 87). In fact, the net benefit of tourism investment could be considerably reduced if a country chooses to construct large-sized hotels and other prestige projects. Elkan (1975, p. 126-127) found that the larger Kenyan hotels were more expensive to build and had greater costs per bed.

He concluded that small-sized hotels would maximize on hotel employment. Another factor which influences tourism's capacity to generate employment is the amount of imports (including food and drink) which must be brought in on account of tourism. The greater the size of the imports, the smaller the number of jobs resulting from tourism activity.

Summary's (1987) study found that Kenya's tourism industry pays rather low wages. She argues that employment generated in tourism is below what would be expected, considering tourism's share of the gross domestic product. As will become clear below, this is partly because of the structure of the country's tourism industry which is foreign-owned, controlled and managed and which allows some of the employment to be generated abroad.

Direct employment in tourism has been criticized on two grounds: most of it is unskilled and its availability is highly seasonal. Lack of skills and seasonality are very intricately intertwined. Some estimates indicate that 75 percent of workers in tourism have no skills or training for the jobs they do (Gamble, 1989). This is a problem in as far as it affects the level of wages, security of tenure and the ability to influence better working terms and conditions. Also, the quality of productivity is affected by lack of training.

International tourism in Africa tends to be highly seasonal. The majority of the west European and North American tourists visit during the northern hemisphere winter. The numbers begin to dry up in April; the annual cycle commences again in August/September or October. The problem of seasonality affects all tourism destinations, especially those that promote the beach holiday from Tunisia to The Gambia, to Kenya.

During the low season, many employees lose their jobs. In The Gambia, for example, 50 percent of the hotel workers are laid off as the hotels close down between April and October for lack of patronage (Dieke, 1993). In Kenya, residents are encouraged to utilize the hotels at special rates adjusted downwards (Sindiga, 1996a). It is more cost-effective to have guests who pay less than to have beds unoccupied. However, many hotels, especially at the coast, close down for renovations and a number of workers are inevitably kept off the payroll. Gamble (1989, p. 15) provides an overall figure of low-season redundancies for all Africa of 25 percent of the workers. But whether the figure is 25 or 50 percent is not really the issue; many people are affected.

Because of the uncertainty of their employment, the bargaining clout for better terms and conditions of service is considerably reduced. In Kenya, people on casual terms of employment have no medical coverage, no housing allowance, and cannot join a trade union. Many tourism workers tend to be trapped in a cycle of hopelessness.

For semi-skilled, supervisory and management positions, tourism enterprises may not employ local people. Tourism businesses, competing to meet international standards to attract the institutionalized tourism market, may look for readily trained people. Such people may not necessarily come from the area in which a tourism enterprise is established, and this can generate conflicts with the indigenous people (Eastman, 1995). In the local eyes, it is another instance of outsiders exploiting local resources for profit, while giving back virtually nothing. This denies tourism the goodwill of local communities. It does not speak well for an industry which is notoriously foreign-dominated in its management and ownership ranks.

Questions have been raised about the quality of jobs available for the local people in the tourism industry. Charges have been made, and rightly so, that the jobs are menial and tend to be servile (Bachmann, 1988; Sindiga, 1994). This has led to negative comments about tourism as "a final form of colonialism" where indigenous people are exploited by outsiders (Middleton, 1992, p. 53). Such jobs include working as porters, labourers, gardeners, drivers, waiters, and so on. In contrast, jobs requiring skills and professional training tend to be held by expatriates. Beyond this, hotel workers in particular are expected to conform to alien attitudes and practices, sometimes against their own cultural values and norms (Bachmann, 1988). But what are the merits of these criticisms?

Whatever jobs are available will be open to those who wish to take up the positions. What, however, is at issue is that supervisory and management positions should be equally open for competition among the residents who possess the required skills. It is important to point this out because key positions in hotels and other tourism enterprises are not filled by expatriates because local people are not capable of performing the tasks. Rather, it is because of the mistaken belief that the expatriates would raise the standard of service (Dieke, 1994, p. 62; Harrell-Bond and Harrell-Bond, 1979).

In The Gambia, a World Bank/United Nations Development Programme plan of 1973 provided for a progressive increase of expatriates in the development of

Gambian tourism, on the assumption that they would provide the expertise which local people "ostensibly lacked" (Harrell-Bond and Harrell-Bond, 1979). This plan was based on wrong notions about Africa and Africans. Over the longer term, plans which exclude local people are not sustainable. As for the conflict of cultures between hotel workers and tourists, this is an inevitable consequence of choosing to work in tourism. Tourists come from varied backgrounds, hold divergent views, and visit for many different reasons. Their encounters with local people are somewhat business-like, rather than personal. Contact between tourists and local people can become smoother through sensitizing both the guests and hosts about mutual respect.

Finally, there is the question of employment and gender in the tourism industry. Most of the workers in various sub-sectors of the industry tend to be men (Elkan, 1975). If this is true, it is a matter which merits further inquiry to discover the underlying reasons. Among Muslims, culture and tradition may preclude women from serving in tourism (Sindiga, 1996b).

Government revenue

Perhaps a significant net gain from the resources generated by tourism accrues as government revenue. This is collected from licensing fees levied on tourism enterprises, and income tax from both the businesses and their employees. Government also obtains excise and customs duties on various tourism-related imports such as capital equipment, vehicles, and drinks. There is also sales tax on the purchase of domestic goods.

Another net gain from tourism income is the wages paid to local staff. Finally, a country may draw a share of surpluses generated by tourism. The domestic share of gross operating surplus will, however, depend on such factors as ownership of the facility, rate of interest on loans, infrastructure costs, tax rates and management fees (Green, 1979). Many countries derive small or no surpluses because of the foreign ownership and management of the majority of the tourism enterprises.

Tourism and regional development

The spatial or regional dimension of development is a way of assessing the impact of a phenomenon on people in a locale at various scales. This idea focuses on whether tourism induces positive externalities for enhanced and balanced economic development in the country. The regional approach is useful for gauging the level of development using specific indicators. Ultimately, a pattern emerges which shows the differential impact of development across the landscape. This can then be used to make effective interventions at the local, regional or national level.

In virtually all the countries of Africa, tourism is spatially concentrated. Deliberately or unwittingly, tourism tends to be developed in enclaves separated from local communities. In these enclaves the tourists lead their own lives in self-contained establishments with hotels, bars, discotheques, swimming pools, massage parlours, indoor sports and other conveniences. Sometimes the tourists' contact with local people is only through the attendants. In short, a kind of western ghetto is created to meet the requirements of the mass or institutional tourist who would like to enjoy his/her holiday without being disturbed. This way, tourism in Africa has developed without the participation of the local people. As Poirier and Wright (1993) have noted, the tourism enclave phenomenon makes contact between tourists and indigenous culture to be "packaged rather than spontaneous, contrived rather than original, whether in terms of organized exhibitions or mass-produced artifacts" (p. 162).

In Tunisia, the tourist enclaves are located along the Mediterranean coast. The majority of the hotels are developed around Tunis, along the beaches of Hammamet-Nabeul, and the 'Sahel' and Djerba-Gabes islands (Poirier and Wright, 1993). In Egypt, tourism is centered on Luxor, a place of outstanding archaeological ruins on the River Nile; Cairo, Aswan, Abu Simbel, Alexandria, Suez, Sinai and Hurghada (Gamble, 1989). In The Gambia, tourism is restricted to the Atlantic ocean beaches near Banjul. And in Kenya, tourism is concentrated along the coast, especially at Mombasa, Malindi, Nairobi, and upcountry national parks and reserves.

The spatial concentration of tourism leads to a similar pattern in the distribution of available jobs. Because of the seasonal nature of the employment, only people who are close by are able to cash in on this. But this need not be so, especially in a country such as Kenya with intensive mobility and circulation of people across the national economic space.

Tourism has sometimes opened up remote places by providing infrastructure such as roads, piped water, electricity, communication lines and by developing accommodation facilities. This may not always be articulated to serve local population centres (Sindiga, 1996b). However, the Kenyan coastal ports of Malindi and Lamu, which had been on the decline for several centuries, were revived by a thriving tourist industry over the past four decades (Middleton, 1992; Sindiga 1996b; Bachmann, 1988).

In Kenya, the impact of tourism on regional development at the national level is only modest. As noted above, tourism is concentrated in the two cities of Nairobi and Mombasa, along the Indian ocean coast and in the national parks. Some 80 percent of the tourist accommodation is located in areas where only 10 percent of the country's population lives; in addition, most of the transportation business is concentrated in Nairobi and Mombasa (Bachmann 1988, p. 167).

Minimizing Leakages and Negative Effects

It is difficult to make a definitive assessment of tourism's impact on African development because planning for tourism is very weak. Except perhaps for Tunisia (Gant and Smith, 1992; Poirier and Wright, 1993), there is no serious sectoral planning for tourism in any African country (Lea, 1993; Green 1979). Even in Kenya, in spite of a relatively strong tourist industry, the assessment made about two decades ago is still largely true.

Kenya's sectoral planning for tourism is weak, in marked contrast to its good negotiating ability and its high strategic ambitions for the sector (Green, 1979, p. 97). Because sectoral planning is weak, "no rational evaluation of a tourism strategy can be made without knowledge of the goals it is intended to further and alternative ways of furthering them" (Green, 1979, p. 99).

Very frequently, national plans show lists of "hoped for outcomes" in the tourism sector rather than an agenda for implementation (Lea, 1993, p. 74). The Kenya government statements, for example, call for one million tourists in the year 2000 but do not go beyond that to say what will be done once that number has been attained. Also, they do not specify how the desired tourist arrivals relate to national development objectives. Planning for tourism serves a number of other purposes: minimizing potential conflicts with competing land uses; developing desired tourism; and projecting its impact on environment and society now and in the future (*ibid.,* 1993). In order for tourism to be sustainable, its planning must be based on local capacities and community perspectives, without which it cannot succeed (Murphy, 1985).

Planning requires baseline information about the tourism sector, its history, its functioning, how it has been changing over time, its performance potential for further development and how optimal benefits can be obtained (Lea, 1993; Green

1979). Only in this way can the positive and negative contributions of tourism be pinpointed with a view to formulating policies and projects which could enhance the positive role and ameliorate the negative consequences.

Also, regions of tourism concentration experience certain negative socio-cultural consequences. The enclave nature of African tourism development takes western culture to remote communities which may have unviable livelihood systems. Soon, the indigenous people are encouraged to enter into some kind of patron-client relationship to make money or to escape from their objective material circumstances. Migot-Adholla *et.al.* (1992, p. 88-89) noted that such relationships may range from begging, posing for photographs, performing dance routines, to casual or organized sex, all for money. At the Kenya coast, especially at Watamu, youths are increasingly dropping out of school and engaging in antisocial behaviour including alcohol consumption, loitering, theft and other petty crime; others are hawking souvenirs and crafts along the beach (Sindiga, 1996b; Beckerleg, 1995; Peake, 1989). The beach boys, as these youths are popularly known, offer services as male prostitutes for female or male clients, companionship, tour-guiding and the like (Peake, 1989).

Instead of regional development, tourism can lead to regional resentment. Tourist behaviour such as scant dressing, public displays of affection between the sexes, and so on, may clash with local tradition and culture and can result in local opposition to the tourism industry. Tourists become purveyors of the negative aspects of western culture. These problems could be minimized or mitigated with careful planning and management (Inskeep, 1991).

CONCLUSION

This chapter has shown the complexity of assessing the impact of tourism on a continental scale. Both the levels of returns from and the impact of tourism on the society and the environment are heavily influenced by government policies and types of tourism. Foreign exchange receipts and employment opportunities, for example, diminish considerably with large-scale developments in the tourism industry which lead to a large volume of imports. The impacts of tourism on space over time and among social groups are highly variegated.

Development is about change – behavioural, attitudinal, social, cultural, economic and even political. Every development effort must bring about change. Although much has been written about the impacts of tourism among host communities, most of the literature is cast in a negative mode, frequently depicting Third World people as static and therefore requiring protection from tourism. Moreover, most of the existing knowledge on the impacts of tourism tends to be generalized. In order to understand tourism's many impacts, detailed typologies of tourism and tourists and the nature of guest-host interactions must be delineated (Wall, 1996) along the lines suggested by Valene Smith (1977). Only then can a meaningful analysis be done on the impact of tourism in Africa.

Tourism's contribution to the African economy appears to be frequently overestimated. The structure, organization and management of international tourism favours transnational corporations from the developed world, assuring a very large outflow of the resources generated by tourism in Africa. When the leakages of foreign exchange are discounted, plus the local resources invested in tourism, the net impact is rather small. This situation could be ameliorated by strict sectoral planning of tourism development. However, planning alone is not sufficient, there must be a political will on the part of African bureaucrats to implement the provisions of tourism planning to ensure their countries obtain maximum benefits from tourism. Of course, an arrangement that guarantees African countries an equitable share of tourism's revenues could discourage rather than encourage transnational corporations from investing in tourism in Africa. That is a challenge.

Tourism employment has generated a lot of interest because only subordinate jobs tend to go to the local people, with the supervisory and management positions going to expatriates. The popular but erroneous explanation for this arrangement is that Africans have not been trained to take up senior ranks in tourism. The problem, however, is that there are usually no plans to reverse the matter. Transnational companies keep a large expatriate management staff component as part of their agreement to work in Africa. As they usually control the tourism enterprises, this cannot be reversed. The answer to the problem would be a structural change of the ownership and control of tourism businesses in Africa to allow the progressive entry of local people into the management arena. In a number of African countries, notably Kenya, a cadre of university-trained tourism professionals now exists (Sindiga, 1996c). These people should be given the opportunity to manage Africa's tourism industry.

This chapter has also shown that tourism's meagre benefits to the African economy could be improved by regional cooperation and intra-Africa tourism. Multi-destination packaging and marketing undertaken by a number of countries can offer varied attractions, giving tourists the opportunity to choose what they would like to see. Besides, the contemporary trend in tourism emphasizes multi-destination travelling. For the host countries it is cheaper and more cost-effective to promote and market a region rather than a single country.

Regional cooperation in tourism can be done within the framework of Africa's many sub-regional groupings. Despite the proliferation of such economic communities, however, there has been relatively little market integration in Africa. Borders of African countries are difficult to cross because of a myriad of administrative barriers which hinder regional tourism development.

Tourism is well developed in only a few African countries and attracts visitors mainly from developed countries. Except perhaps in Southern Africa, intra-Africa tourism could be enhanced by a more positive attitude and pride of the African peoples about their own continent. Successful intra-Africa tourism could be achieved with greater interaction of the African peoples at the personal, professional, trade, national and regional levels.

ENDNOTES

1. This chapter is taken from my manuscript entitled "Tourism and African Development: Change and Challenge of Tourism in Kenya" (Leiden, African Studies Centre, forthcoming). The initial preparation of this study was done when I was a Visiting Research Fellow at the African Studies Centre, Leiden, The Netherlands in 1997. I am grateful to the ASC for its assistance.

2. Inexplicably, the WTO excludes Egypt and Libya from the North Africa tourism sub-region. These figures therefore do not reflect tourism activity in those countries, both of which are included in the Middle East.

3. South Africa should rightly be called Southern Africa to reflect the geographical location but the WTO does not appear to follow that convention. The countries represented are Botswana, Lesotho, Namibia, South Africa and Swaziland. It may be noted also that the majority of the tourists in Southern Africa appear to represent movements within the region rather than from outside the African continent. Such tourists appear to spend less money than those from outside Africa. This is the probable accounting for the relatively low receipts for South Africa, Zimbabwe and Botswana in relation to the numbers of arrivals as shown on Table 1.5. These trends are discussed below under the section on intra-Africa tourism.

4. This might be true in a relative sense. Kenya, however, experiences serious leakages with packaged all-inclusive beach tourism involving little or no local travel within the country (Kenya, 1991; Sindiga, 1994). Also, there are heavy leakages in international air travel because most tourists travel in chartered and scheduled foreign airlines (Sinclair, 1990; Sinclair et.al., 1992; Sindiga, 1996a).

5. A vigorous debate on the role of tourism in Tanzania's socialist development was conducted through that country's media in 1970 (Shivji, 1975). Suffice to note here that under the Arusha declaration of 1967 which moved the country to the left, Tanzania saw tourism as being incompatible with its socialist ideology. Specifically, the country appeared to protest the presence of rich visitors, a perception which would dramatize the inequality between guests and hosts thereby exposing Tanzanians to capitalist forms of consumption. Also, it would undermine cultural life and allegedly destroy wildlife (Kahama, 1995). In addition, Tanzania's tourist industry was put under the direction of an inefficient public sector which was not sensitized to the importance of facility development and maintenance. Tourism was also impeded by huge bureaucratic procedures at airports and other entry points and even at state banks where it took two hours to obtain bank change. As Kahama (1995) notes, an overvalued local currency made tourism too expensive. By 1973, investments in tourism had virtually ceased. Further, Tanzania closed its border with Kenya between 1977 and 1983. Under the circumstances, most tourists to East Africa started and completed their holidays in Kenya. As a general observation, the inflexibility of the heavily centralized state bureaucracies in socialist systems makes it difficult to do the business of international tourism (Hall, 1992).

REFERENCES

Achebe, C. 1984: *The Trouble with Nigeria. Nairobi:* Heinemann Kenya.

Bachmann, P. 1988: *Tourism in Kenya: A Basic Need for Whom?* European University Studies 10. Berne: Peter Lang.

Beckerleg, S. 1995: 'Brown Sugar' or Friday Prayers: Youth Choices and Community Building in Coastal Kenya. *African Affairs,* 94 (374), 23-38.

Brohman, J. 1996: New Directions in Tourism for Third World Development. *Annals of Tourism Research,* 23 (1), 48-70.

Christian Aid. 1995: *An Abuse of Innocence: Tourism and Child Prostitution in the Third World.* London: Christian Aid.

Courier, The. 1988: *The Courier,* (112), (November - December).

Curry, S. 1982: The Terms of Trade and Real Import Capacity of the Tourism Sector in Tanzania. *Journal of Development Studies,* 18 (4), 479-496.

de Kadt, E. 1976: Tourism: Passport to Development: Perspectives on the Social and Cultural Effects of Tourism in Developing Countries. New York: Oxford.

Dieke, P.U.C. 1993: Tourism Policy and Employment in the Gambia. *Employee Relations,* (15), 71-80.

Dieke, P.U.C. 1994: The Political Economy of Tourism in the Gambia. *Review of African Political Economy,* 21 (62), 611-627.

Dieke, P.U.C. 1995: Tourism and Structural Adjustment Programmes in the African Economy. *Tourism Economics,* 1 (1), 71-93.

Eastman, C.M. 1995: Tourism in Kenya and the Marginalization of Swahili. *Annals of Tourism Research,* 22 (1), 172-185.

Elkan, W. 1975: The Relation Between Tourism and Employment in Kenya and Tanzania. *Journal of Development Studies,* 11 (2), 123-130.

Ellis, S. and MacGaffey, J. 1996: Research on Sub-Sahara's Unrecorded International Trade: Some Methodological and Conceptual Problems. *African Studies Review,* 39 (2), 19-45.

Gamble, W.P. 1989: *Tourism and Development in Africa.* London: John Murray.

Gant, R. and Smith, J. 1992: Tourism and National Development Planning in Tunisia. *Tourism Management,* 13 (3), 331-336.

Green, R.H. 1979: Toward Planning Tourism in African Countries. In Emanuel de Kadt (ed.), *Tourism: Passport to Development?,* pp. 79-100. New York: Oxford.

Hall, D.R. 1992: Tourism Development in Cuba. In David Harrison (ed.), *Tourism and the Less Developed Countries,* pp. 102-120. London: Belhaven Press.

Harrell-Bond, B.E. and Harrell-Bond, D.L. 1979: Tourism in the Gambia. *Review of African Political Economy,* 14, 78-90.

Inskeep, E. 1991: *Tourism Planning: An Integrated and Sustainable Development Approach.* New York: van Nostrand Reinhold.

Kahama, C.G. 1995: *Tanzania into the 21st Century.* Dar es Salaam: Tema Publishers.

Kenya, Republic of. 1991: *Development and Employment in Kenya: A Strategy for the Transformation of the Economy* – Report of the Presidential Committee on Employment. Nairobi: Government Printer.

Lea, J.P. 1981: Changing Approaches Towards Tourism in Africa: Planning and Research Perspectives. *Journal of Contemporary African Studies,* 1, 19-40.

Lea, J.P. 1993: *Tourism and Development in the Third World.* London and New York: Routledge.

Middleton, J. 1992: *The World of the Swahili: An African Mercantile Civilization.* New Haven and London: Yale University Press.

Migot-Adholla, S.E., Mkangi, K.G.C., Mbindyo, J., Mulaa, J.K. and Opinya, N.O. 1992: Study of Tourism in Kenya with Emphasis on the Altitudes of Residents of the Kenya Coast. *IDS Consultancy Reports,* 7. Nairobi: University of Nairobi, Institute for Development Studies.

Mitchell, F. 1970: The Value of Tourism in East Africa. *Eastern Africa Economic Review,* 2 (1), 1-21.

Murphy, P.E. 1985: *Tourism: A Community Approach.* New York and London: Routledge.

Namibia, Republic of. no date listed. *First National Development Plan (NDP 1) Volume 1: 1995/1996 -1999/2000.* Windhoek: National Planning Commission.

Ndiaye, B. 1990: Prospects for Economic Integration in Africa. In Anyang' Nyong'o (ed.), *Regional Integration in Africa: Unfinished Agenda,* pp. 35-41. Nairobi: Academy Science Publishers.

Nyong'o, A. (ed.). 1990: *Regional Integration in Africa: Unfinished Agenda.* Nairobi: Academy Science Publishers.

Peake, R. 1989: Swahili Stratification and Tourism in Malindi Old Town, Kenya. *Africa,* 59 (2), 209-220.

Poirier, R.A. and Wright, S. 1993: The Political Economy of Tourism in Tunisia. *Journal of Modern African Studies,* 31(1), 149-162.

Popovic, V. 1972: *Tourism in Eastern Africa.* Munich: Weltforum Verlag.

Richter, Linda K. 1992: Political Instability and Tourism in the Third World. In David Harrison (ed.), *Tourism and the Less Developed Countries,* pp. 35-46. London: Belhaven Press.

Sharpley, R., Sharpley, J. and Adams, J. 1996: Travel Advice or Trade Embargo? The Impacts and Implications of Official Travel Advice. *Tourism Management,* 17 (1), 1-7.

Shivji, I. (ed.). 1975: *Tourism and Socialist Development.* Dar es Salaam: Tanzania Publishing House.

Sinclair, N.T. 1990: *Tourism Development in Kenya.* Consultancy Report. Nairobi: World Bank.

Sinclair, M.T., Alizadeh, P. and Onunga, E.A.A. 1992: The Structure of International Tourism and Tourism Development in Kenya. In David Harrison (ed.), *Tourism and the Less Developed Countries*, pp. 47-63. London: Belhaven Press.

Sindiga, I. 1994: Employment and Training in Tourism in Kenya. *Journal of Tourism Studies*, 5 (2), 45-52.

Sindiga, I. 1996a: Domestic Tourism in Kenya. *Annals of Tourism Research*, 23 (1), 19-31.

Sindiga, I. 1996b: International Tourism in Kenya and the Marginalization of the Waswahili. *Tourism Management*, 17 (6), 425-432.

Sindiga, I. 1996c: Tourism Education in Kenya. *Annals of Tourism Research*, 23 (3), 698-701.

Smith, V.L. 1977: Introduction. In Valene L. Smith (ed.), *Hosts and Guests: the Anthropology of Tourism*, pp. 1-14. Philadelphia: University of Pennsylvania.

Summary, R. 1987: Tourism's Contribution to the Economy of Kenya. *Annals of Tourism Research*, 14, 531-540.

Teye, V.B. 1991: Prospects for Regional Tourism Cooperation in Africa. In S. Medlik (ed.), *Managing Tourism*, pp. 286-296. Oxford: Butterworth-Heinemann Ltd.

United Nations Economic Commission for Africa. 1989: *African Alternative Framework to Structural Adjustment Programmes for Socio-Economic Recovery and Transformation*. Addis Ababa: UNECA.

Wall, G. 1996: Rethinking Impacts of Tourism. *Progress in Tourism and Hospitality Research*, 2, 207-215.

Williams, A.V. 1976: Tourism. In C.G. Knight and J.L. Newman (eds.), *Contemporary Africa: Geography and Change*, pp. 457-465. Englewood Cliffs, New Jersey: Prentice Hall.

World Bank. 1989: *Sub-Saharan Africa: From Crisis to Sustainable Growth: A Long-Term Perspective Study*. Washington D.C.: World Bank.

World Bank. 1991: *World Development Report 1991:The Challenge of Development*. New York: Oxford.

Chapter 2

DEFINING ECOTOURISM

by Donald G. Reid

INTRODUCTION

Ecotourism is a term that is quickly being adopted by many tourism enterprises, whether their activity is driven by values of conservation and preservation or not. The term connotes notions of sustainablility which all in the enterprise, either those served or the servers, can embrace. It is often referred to as the feel-good term which, in fact, can hide many sins. As Jaakson (1997, p.33) states "the popularity of ecotourism has backfired and the term 'ecotourism' has become jargon. 'Ego-tourism' has become a word-play on 'eco-tourism'."

Tourism is often seen as a benign activity by individuals and groups interested in preserving the world's remaining natural lands and wildlife from the alternate uses to which those resources could be allocated. It is quickly becoming recognized, however, that it may not be true that tourism activities are less damaging to the environment than the alternatives. Many tourism enterprises in so-called protected areas have a profound negative effect on the environment, as well as the local people and their culture.

Other tourism enterprises, however, are sincerely interested in the environmental situations that confront the human community and are attempting to introduce principles of environmental conservation in their activities. The world of tourism has witnessed a move away from the gun to the camera over the last few decades. There is a growing understanding among hosts and guests alike, that the resource base on which tourism depends must be protected if these sites are to last over the long term. Many tourists are becoming more sophisticated and reflect an ecological ethic in their needs and desires. In addition, local people and their cultures are gaining recognition as part of the ecosystem and, as a consequence, their welfare is increasingly factored into the equation when considering development of new tourism destinations.

Although there is growing awareness of these issues among individuals, companies and national governments with a natural tourism base, there remains the difficulty of implementing ecotourism principles into actual development. The counter forces to the preservation philosophy described above are compelling circumstances which often influence and direct growth.

Perhaps of most consequence are national governments desperate to raise foreign currency in an attempt to deal with mounting debt. Tourism in many of these countries has become the top foreign currency earner and provides employment opportunities to massive populations always on the brink of unending poverty. Many developing nations are also under great pressure to deregulate markets by the powerful free-market lobby which manifests itself through such international institutions as the International Monetary Fund, the World Trade Organization and the World Bank. Sovereign governments are continually becoming less sovereign in these matters.

Commitment to the preservation philosophy is also countered by a population's lack of basic skills and poorly developed civil institutions which are not able to monitor and evaluate the consequences of unfettered growth. In addition, local communities have often been bypassed as participants in the tourism development process with disastrous results. This matter will be dealt with in greater detail later in this chapter.

THE CONSUMPTIVE/NON-CONSUMPTIVE CONTINUUM

Tourism, no matter how classified, rests on a continuum from highly consumptive to practically non-consumptive (Figure 2.1).

Figure 2.1 Tourism Continuum

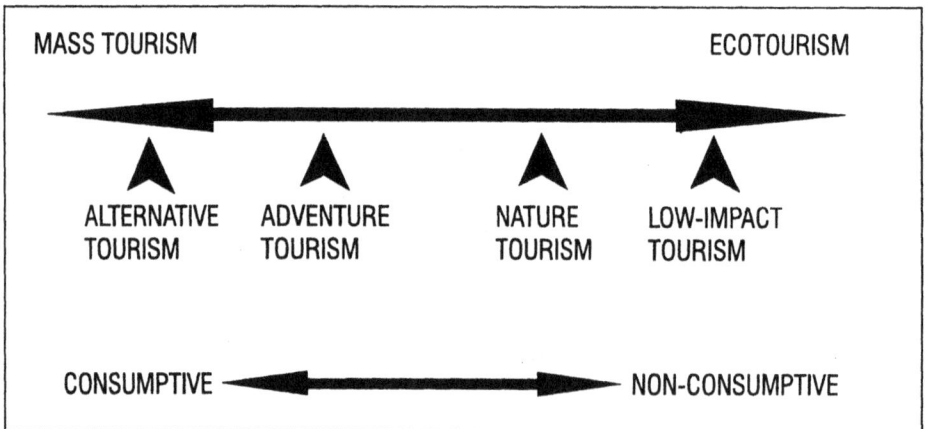

MASS TOURISM   ECOTOURISM

ALTERNATIVE   ADVENTURE   NATURE   LOW-IMPACT
TOURISM   TOURISM   TOURISM   TOURISM

CONSUMPTIVE ←——————————→ NON-CONSUMPTIVE

Whether an activity is consumptive or not depends on the frame of mind with which implementation is approached. Some activities are designated consumptive simply by their very nature. Hunting, for example, is considered highly consumptive. However, some argue that at certain periods, when herds continue to procreate beyond what the ecosystem can support, it is in the best interest of bio-diversity to cull the herd. Generally speaking, however, hunting without this larger frame of reference is by its very nature, ultimately, a highly consumptive activity.

The polar opposites of the tourism experience and its organization can be displayed at each end of the continuum. Mass tourism tends to be generated and driven without regard for conservation issues and, in fact, promotes the highest levels of consumption possible. This form of tourism is very legitimate depending on the circumstances and environment in which it is carried out. Disney World, for example, is intended to be a highly consumptive activity and is constructed in such a manner that it has little impact on the environment beyond the support capability of the local infrastructure and services. At the other extreme is the fragile ecosystem which may be the only one of its kind left in the world. Here, attempts are made to restrict use to non-consumptive activities which may mean they are not available to the general public except through mass media or other artificial means. All other activities fall somewhere on the continuum between these two poles.

For students of tourism, the great difficulty is to determine how to describe and classify activities accurately on the continuum. Figure 2.1 attempts to present a crude allocation of activities on the continuum, but it is only meant to be a starting point of the debate and not an attempt at a definitive typology.

While description and classification are not predominant activities of a domain of study more concerned with the issues of implementation and management, they are nevertheless crucial subjects if tourism development is to be a true alternative to the more consumptive uses of the natural resource base. Description and classification are necessary if ecotourism is to be legitimized and not used as a catchall phrase in inappropriate situations.

The other designations on the continuum presented in Figure 2.1 also require some definition.

Alternative tourism is an attempt by scholars and practitioners alike to modify the mass tourism experience. While not necessarily reducing its consumptive nature, it does reduce the size and density of the setting while providing the same

31

experience – usually sun, sand and surf – in a more tranquil manner. This density reduction can have positive environmental effects, but still does not qualify the activity as ecotourism. For example, for many tourists, a small, secluded country inn nestled in a less dense area may be preferable to the large hotel on the beach.

Adventure tourism is a term which has been coined to signify that the activity being pursued has a certain amount of risk to it. This type of activity often takes place in the natural environment. However, gambling, which is usually conducted indoors, may also be classified as adventure tourism.

Nature tourism is generally defined as activities likely to be more passive in their confrontation with the environment. They may, however, be philosophically more consumptive than low-impact tourism in that they are pursued for accumulative purposes, even if it may be something as environmentally benign as the identification of bird species. Often in the pursuit of this kind of goal, other aspects of the environment are disrupted and damaged. Low-impact tourism is often pursued without actually entering the environment or disrupting species. If the area is entered, it is done so with a minimum of damage occurring; this can be accomplished by viewing a setting from some distance.

What distinguishes the foregoing classes or types of activities is their treatment of the environment and the natural resource base. On the consumptive side, the environment is seen as an 'object' through which the recreational activities are played out. For example, a mountain is seen as an obstacle to be overcome through climbing, rather than as an aesthetic and ecological marvel to behold. On the non-consumptive side, the natural resource base is considered by the participant as the 'subject', to be viewed, studied and analyzed. The ecotourism activity, in this instance, is one in which the participant studies, views and analyzes the natural environment in a non-consumptive mode. It is recognized that complete non-consumption is not likely ever reached, but the primary motivation is not physical consumption. For example, the mountain referred to earlier may be painted by an amateur artist for purposes of intimate, intrinsic and spiritual examination without intrusion. This example demonstrates that what constitutes ecotourism needs continued and more detailed clarification.

Defining Ecotourism

A small number of scholars have been attempting to define ecotourism for some time. Ceballos-Lacurain (in Ziffer, 1989) suggests that:

> Ecological tourism implies a scientific, aesthetic or philosophical approach, although the ecological tourist is not required to be a professional scientist, artist or philosopher. The main point is that the person who practices ecotourism has the opportunity of immersing him or herself in nature in a way most people cannot enjoy in their routine, urban existence. This person will eventually acquire a consciousness that will convert him/her into somebody keenly involved in conservation issues (p. 5).

Boo (1990) and Lindberg (1991) define ecotourism as tourism that involves traveling to relatively undisturbed or uncontaminated nature areas with the specific objective of studying, admiring and enjoying the scenery and its wild plants and animals, as well as any existing cultural areas. Scace, et.al., (1992) and Wight (1994) also suggest that ecotourism is nature travel that actually contributes to conservation. Wight (ibid., pp. 39-40) provides the following principles on which the ecotourism experience must be constructed:

- it should not degrade the resource and should be developed in an environmentally sound manner;
- it should provide long-term benefits to the resource, to local community and industry (benefits may be conservation, scientific, social, cultural, or economic);
- it should provide first-hand, participatory and enlightening experiences;
- it should involve education among all parties – local communities, government, non-governmental organizations, industry and tourists (before, during and after the trip);
- it should encourage all-party recognition of the intrinsic values of the resource;
- it should involve acceptance of the resource on its own terms, and in recognition of its limits, which involves supply-oriented management;
- it should involve understanding and involve partnerships between many players, which could include government, non-governmental organizations, industry, scientists and locals (both before and during operations);
- it should promote moral and ethical responsibilities and behaviours towards the natural and cultural environment by all players.

Boo (1990) continues on to say that ecotourism development is the process of change to reach a symbiosis between nature conservation, sustainable socio-economic development and nature tourism.

Perhaps an even more compelling ingredient in this definition is the notion of 'spirituality' which Jaakson (1997) introduces into the discussion. He suggests that many of the definitions of ecotourism leave out the human component which is the spiritual. Jaakson (*ibid.*) suggests:

> An insistent equating of ecotourism with nature overshadows a human dimension of deep spirituality which I speculate is the motivation, consciousness or subconscious, for all ecotourism travel. This spirituality is akin to the travel of devout pilgrims to worship at sacred and holy sites. Ecotourism in pristine natural sites is a form of secular pilgrimage where nature is the sacred holy site. The premise here is that the essence of ecotourism is an <u>ethic</u> that makes ecotourism different from other types of tourism (p. 34).

One additional consideration needs to be raised when discussing the meaning of ecotourism. That consideration is the definition of rural tourism, given that most, if not all, ecotourism occurs in the countryside or in small settlements. Reid, Fuller, and Haywood (1995, p. 23) suggest:

> Rural tourism is distinguishable by its projection of traditional (authentic or unauthentic) rural life into the attractions which constitute its core. It is generally constructed around the built or natural environment and includes programs such as festivals and cultural activities which often reenact or provide a flavour of the traditional local or rural culture and history.

While rural tourism quite often reconstructs either natural or human made environments that have been destroyed, ecotourism would not likely participate in reconstructed or artificial interpretations of natural phenomena unless it was for the purposes of study or education.

HUMAN COMMUNITIES AS AN ESSENTIAL INGREDIENT IN ECOTOURISM

So far in this chapter, the discussion of ecotourism has focused on the natural environment and the experience of the tourist. What is often overlooked in ecotourism development is the involvement of the local community and its culture. In fact, local culture, particularly in developing countries, is often part of the ecotourism product but not necessarily considered when benefits from that product are being disbursed. However, it is quickly becoming recognized that to neglect rural communities, which are part of the natural environment and the ecosystem, is to neglect a large part of the ecotourism system itself. If not completely left out of tourism development, rural communities are asked to be involved at the implementation stage – but rarely at the beginning stage of the planning process.

Proponents of ecotourism, as a sustainable and viable alternative to more exploitive uses of the natural resource base, have been quick to recognize that active involvement in the decision-making process by those who will be most affected is a critical component of successful and sustainable tourism development. Furthermore, it is equally recognized that benefits from this development must flow to the affected community as well as to the other actors in the system. The time has passed when people living at or near the development can be completely ignored, no matter how important the project may appear to be from the national or private perspective.

Often, ecotourism activities are designed to replace traditional economic practices and are foreign to the local inhabitants. Integration of ecotourism into the dominant culture of the area, if thought desirable, needs to be planned using a grass roots approach rather than being imposed from the outside. If we expect people to change their lifestyle to accommodate new enterprise, their active involvement in the design and management of that project change is crucial. Some may argue that the basic decision to change historical practices should not be stimulated by outside forces at all, but should be left entirely to the local community. Additionally, a fundamental principle of ecotourism development must be to direct a good share of the benefits emanating from the project to the local area and to keep leakage of those benefits to a minimum. Often, what is considered to be a benefit at the macro level turns out to be negative at the micro level.

Given the present trends in today's global economy, however, these principles may be no longer realistic. At the present time, perhaps the best that can be hoped for is the full engagement of the local people to discuss the project's feasibility and its desirable effects on the community and environment.

Proponents of ecotourism are learning that active engagement of local people in the planning process is a complex issue and not just a matter of selling communities on outside intentions. At its most fundamental level, it involves mutual learning and partnership development between local people and outside agents. Often, what gets passed off as participatory planning is pure manipulation of the local population by the outside planning and development agent. While this may not be the original intent of the planning process, it often occurs because of the planners' lack of skills in community development practice or because of the historic relationship between the planning institution and the local community. This may be particularly true for peoples who have been subjected to colonial relationships such as those in many Eastern and Southern African countries. Old patterns continue even though new political systems, initiated to overcome these barriers, are being implemented.

THE COMMUNITY DEVELOPMENT APPROACH TO ECOTOURISM DEVELOPMENT

There are too many theoretical approaches of community development to review adequately here (see Freidmann, 1969; Reid and van Dreunen, 1996; Rotheman, 1974; Wharfe, 1992). However, some discussion is warranted given the practice of many planning institutions to allocate employees with limited training in this approach to manage ecotourism development with communities. Perhaps the first principle should be to train staff in community development practice so they can guide communities through a satisfactory process.

At the most basic level, community development practice is not essentially concerned with implementing a particular project, in this case ecotourism development, but is fundamentally designed to educate people through the process, forging the community's capacity to facilitate lasting community autonomy and strength. Reid and van Dreunen (1996, p. 49) suggest that community development "is a process for empowerment and transformation" of individuals and communities. The objective of community development is to build individual skills and community solidarity. It encourages the community's self-reliance and builds confidence in the community's ability to control its ultimate destiny. In a pure community development approach, the chief goal is to increase the capacity of the community using a concrete project such as the development of an ecotourism destination.

All too often, the planners' chief objective is the ecotourism project itself, and community involvement becomes the method for achieving that objective. This usually occurs because the community has become a stumbling block to a proposed development and must be dealt with in some way. Of course, it makes for a much cleaner process to focus initially on the community and its needs, out of which the potential of an ecotourism project may be realized. Through a community development approach to planning, not only is the end product likely to be planned more comprehensively in the final analysis, but it is also likely to have greater local community support and lasting commitment than if planned using a more streamlined, top-down approach.

Engaging the community in ecotourism development can proceed on many levels. Arnstein (1969) has presented a model of citizen participation which describes the various approaches.

Figure 2.2 Levels of Citizen Participation

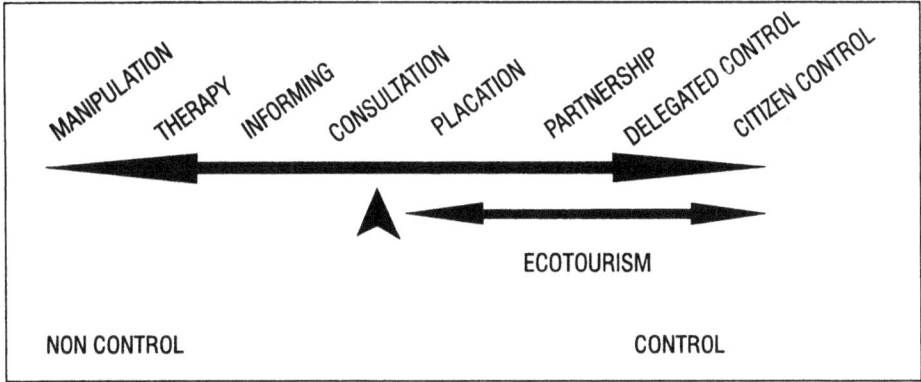

Source: Arnstein, 1969

This model suggests that community involvement in decision-making can stretch the continuum from pure outright manipulation on the part of the planning agent, to absolute community control of decision-making. In all likelihood, an ecotourism project will fall somewhere in the middle of this continuum. However, it would be difficult to characterize any project as ecotourism if the point of engagement is situated left of the mid-point on the continuum as indicated in Figure 2.2.

REFERENCES

Arnstein, S. 1969: A Ladder of Citizen Participation. *Journal of the American Institute of Planners*, 4, 216-224.

Boo, E. 1990: *Ecotourism: The Potentials and Pitfalls*. Maryland: World Wildlife Fund.

Freidmann, J. 1969: *Planning in the Public Domain: from knowledge to action*. Princeton: Princeton University Press.

Jaakson, R. 1997: Exploring the Epistemology of Ecotourism. *Journal of Applied Recreation Research*, Vol. 22, No 1.

Lindberg, K. 1991: *Policies for Maximizing Nature Tourism's Ecological and Economic Benefits*. Washington: World Resources Institute.

Reid, D. and van Dreunen, L. 1996: Leisure as a Social Transformation Mechanism in Community Development Practice. *Journal of Applied Recreation Research*, 21, (1).

Reid, D., Fuller, A.M. and Haywood, K.M. 1995: Tourism: Saviour or False Hope for the Rural Economy? *Plan Canada*, 35, (3).

Rotheman, J. 1974: Three Models of Community Organization Practice. In Fred Cox et. al. (eds.), *Strategies of Community Organization, 2nd edition*. Itasca: Peacock Press.

Scace, R., Grifone, E. and Usher, R. 1992: *Ecotourism in Canada*. Ottawa: Canadian Environmental Advisory Council, Supply and Services Canada.

Wharfe, B. 1992: *Communities and Social Policy in Canada*. Toronto: McClelland & Stewart Inc.

Wight, P. 1994: Environmentally Responsible Marketing of Tourism. In *Ecotourism: A Sustainable Option?* Chichester: John Wiley & Sons.

Ziffer, K. 1989: *Ecotourism: the Uneasy Alliance*. Washington: Conservation International, Ernst and Young.

Chapter 3

COMMUNITY BASED TOURISM IN KWAZULU NATAL: SOME CONCEPTUAL ISSUES

by Ray Naguran

INTRODUCTION

South Africa, with its impressive combination of natural and cultural features, has become a popular ecotourism destination for visitors from high-income countries as well as from the more affluent sector of the domestic market. Definitions of ecotourism are still evolving, but generally the concept implies far more than a nature experience. It implies that some benefit remains with the people who are supplying the product without harming the environment or community in the process. It advocates for resource sustainability, economic viability of the tourism product, minimum negative impacts on the environment and the local communities, and the participation of local communities in the economic benefits that flow from tourism activities, a criterion often agreed upon as essential to the condition of sustainability in ecotourism (Handley, 1996).

Tourism in South Africa has a poor history of involving local communities and previously neglected groups in tourist related activities. The essence of South Africa's conservation policies under the apartheid government was largely a programme to select interesting biological complexes and bestow on them a distinct legal status. Although conservation in South Africa was perceived to be successful, there was a large element of failure because rural communities had been bypassed and alienated from the conservation effort (World Bank, 1995). People had been forcibly removed from their land to make way for conservation areas and, as a result, there was much anger and a feeling that animals were thought to be more important than people. Communities had, in the past, regarded themselves as playing no part in tourism and considered themselves merely objects for tourists to view. Dr. George Hughes, acting chief executive of the KwaZulu Natal Nature Conservation Services, suggested that:

[P]rior to South Africa's democratisation, the wildlife movement was little different in its attitudes to the disenfranchised majority, and suffered both censure of the majority and the tragedy of a lack of understanding. The great SA parks were proclaimed to protect our diversity and to allow ecological processes to operate with minimal human impact (Handley, 1996, p. 137).

The history of community resistance to conservation in these areas has coloured perceptions of both tourism and conservation, with both often perceived as threats.

With the advent of democracy in 1994, the challenge facing the country was to develop policies to rectify the imbalances of the past and open up the tourism industry for participation of the hitherto disadvantaged citizens of the country. South Africa's transition to democracy brought with it a philosophical shift toward a more participatory approach to conservation and tourism development aimed at addressing some of the key constraints of past conservation practices. This approach places more emphasis on the need for greater participation by local communities in the development of tourism. Local communities are placed at the centre of conservation decision-making and emphasis is placed on the role of local institutions in the management of natural resources.

Such new approaches to conservation and tourism development, in which the local community derives benefits from conservation, have been increasingly applied in several areas of southern Africa. The CAMPFIRE programme in Zimbabwe and the ADMADE programme in Zambia are two examples. These projects have been collectively referred to in the literature by different designations, for example, community based natural resource management (CBNRM), and integrated conservation and development projects (ICDP), and the term that is favoured in this chapter, community based tourism (CBT) (Taylor, 1996).

As the concept of community participation in tourism in South Africa is still in its infancy, there is a lack of a coherent regional plan for tourism development which specifically caters to community based tourism. The rules of the game with respect to community participation in tourism have never been written. Uncertainty and a lack of guidance have resulted in a number of blockages. Equally, tourism which has been developed, particularly on communal land, has been *ad hoc* and unplanned, without reference to a guiding development framework.

The development of a successful ecotourism strategy depends on a number of crucial elements which must be incorporated into a well planned strategy. This is best done within a conceptual framework for tourism analysis (Culpan, 1987). This chapter proposes a framework within the current context of a lack of development and direction for CBT implementation in the province of KwaZulu Natal. It conceptualizes the various elements that affect community based tourism, and provides a focus for adopting a more integrated approach to the design and implementation of community based tourism projects (see Figure 3.1).

Figure 3.1 Community Based Tourism (CBT): A Conceptual Framework

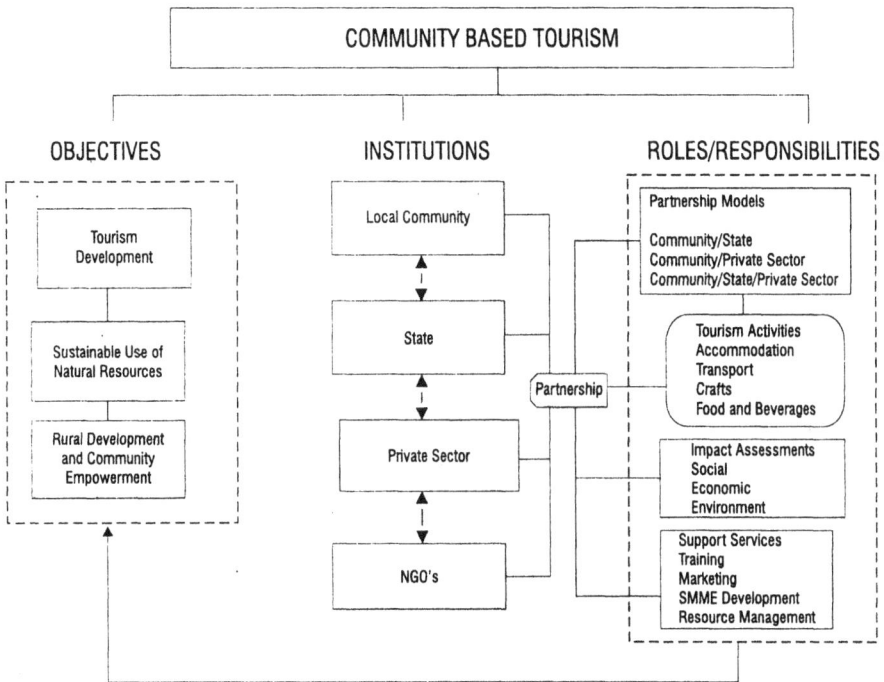

DEFINITIONS

Community based tourism may be defined as the use of a community's resources, both cultural and natural, for tourism activities in order to:

- promote socio-economic development and provide local people with income sources;
- encourage community commitment to conservation of bio-diversity and sustainable management of the natural resource base;
- involve people in the process of their own development and give them more opportunities to participate effectively in development activities.

It includes the community's participation in the design and decision-making process, in the management and administration of tourism and related activities and operations. It ensures a degree of ownership by the community in the development process and operations.

Central to an understanding of community participation is a realization of the variety of meanings and interpretations that people attribute to the concept. Cernea (1991) describes community participation as giving people more opportunities to participate effectively in development activities. These include empowering people to mobilize their own capacities, be social actors rather than passive subjects, manage the resources, make decisions and control the activities which affect their lives.

The concept of community participation has a long history of debate in development circles. The terms "people's participation" and "popular participation" are now part of the normal language of many development agencies including NGOs, government departments and banks (Pimbert & Pretty, 1997).

Pimbert and Pretty (1997) argue that, as in the case of other aspects of rural development, conservation has been characterized by different interpretations of participation. Initially, in the colonial period, people were regarded as an impediment to conservation and management of protected areas was characterized by coercion and control. In the 1970s, participation was adopted as a mechanism to gain the voluntary submission of people in establishing and maintaining conservation areas. In this case, people were passive actors and participation was nothing more than a public relations exercise. A shift occurred during the 1980s when communities began taking an active interest in natural resource protection. Today, participation is regarded as the local people's active involvement in managing a protected area and there is increasing recognition that without this involvement conservation efforts have little chance of success.

The differing interpretations of the term participation are reflected in a typology of participation developed by Jules Pretty (1995). Drawing on the range of ways that development organizations interpret and use the term participation, Pretty has disaggregated participation into seven different types (Table 3.1), allowing for differing degrees of external involvement and local control in the development process. He describes the level of community involvement and offers a critique for each type of participation. The spectrum of participation extends from passive participation, in which local communities possess no power or control over the development process and decisions are made unilaterally by external bodies, to self-mobilization, where local people have complete control over development activities and take initiatives independent of external institutions. In the case of self-mobilization, external consultants provide support services to the community but have no control over the development process. Active participation of local communities in the decision-making process is a characteristic of only the interactive participation and self-mobilization types. It is therefore imperative that when the term participation is used in development, its specific application needs to be clarified, and there should be a shift in focus from the more common passive, consultative and incentive-driven participation towards the interactive end of the spectrum (Pimbert & Pretty, 1997).

Table 3.1 A typology of participation

Typology	Comments
1. Passive Participation	• People participation is limited to being told what is going to or what has already happened • People's responses are not taken into account • Information belongs only to external professionals
2. Participation in information giving	• People participation is limited to provision of information in response to questionnaires, surveys etc. designed by external agents • Findings of the research are not shared with the people – consequently they have no influence on proceedings
3. Participation by consulting	• People participation involves consultation with local people by external agents • The problems and solutions are defined solely by these agents • They may take into account people's views during this process, but are not obliged to do so

4. Participation for material incentives	• People participate by contributing resources (e.g. labour) in return for food, cash or other material incentive • Farmers may provide fields and labour but are not involved in the experimentation or the process of learning • This is often called participation, but people have no stake in prolonging activities when the incentives end
5. Functional participation	• People participate by forming groups to meet specific objectives related to the project • Involvement may be interactive but tends to arise later in the project cycle after major decisions have been made • Institutions formed tend to depend on external facilitators, but may become self dependent
6. Interactive participation	• People participate in joint analysis, development of action plans and creation or strengthening of local institutions • Participation is seen as a right and not only as a means of achieving project goals • It tends to involve interdisciplinary methodologies that seek multiple perspectives and make use of systematic and structured learning processes • Local groups take control of local decision making and determine how resources are to be used giving them a stake in maintaining structures or practices
7. Self-mobilization	• People participate by taking initiatives independent of external institutions or change systems • They develop contacts with external institutions for advice and resources, but retain control of the use of resources • Self-mobilization and collective action may or may not challenge existing inequitable distributions of wealth and power

Source: Pretty (1995)

Commentators on the development and implementation of community based tourism projects agree that institutional relationships and institutional capacity are crucial issues which can affect the success or failure of a project (Jones, 1996). The establishment of partnerships between different institutions and stakeholders in the design and implementation of community based tourism projects is essential for project sustainability. This argument is based on the assumption that community based tourism projects cannot be designed and implemented by one institution or organization acting in isolation. "Partnerships need to be promoted because without coincidence of interests, and joint action to achieve common goals, institutions will not cooperate, and will undermine each other. The relationships between institutions will, to a very large extent, govern the nature of the project and impact heavily on its success or failure" (Jones, 1996, p. 4). The development of a successful community based tourism strategy will require a sound institutional framework based on a constructive partnership between the local community, state, the private sector and NGOs. The next section will focus on the institutional capacity and institutional relationships that are essential components of community based tourism.

Local community

How we define the unit of study has significant implications for participation in development. Participation can be inhibited by the presence of divergent categories of interest within a particular setting. Defining a community can be a complex problem. It is a conglomeration of groups with social and economic differences based on wealth, land, livestock, age, gender, political affiliation, and other factors – differences sometimes too subtle for the outsider to perceive. Therefore, a community cannot be regarded as a homogenous unit, but as something locational. These considerable degrees of contrast help to expose either the influence of a dominant local elite or the need to balance the demands and wishes of different sectors of the community. The concept of one community or the legitimacy of people claiming to speak for the community, may be of limited value. Community leaders may well represent the prevailing power balance, and poor, more marginal people may be poorly represented. It cannot be assumed that the community is a philanthropic social entity concerned with ensuring distributional equity amongst its members. In fact, it is clear that many communities are based on strong principles of hierarchy, the distribution of resources within them being dependent on the place occupied in the hierarchy. Poor households, particularly those headed by females with very young children, are likely to occupy poor position in terms of access to and control of resources (World Bank, 1995).

Definitions of community often do not take into account a wider concept of community, as in a network of interacting small communities. The stereotypical commune was considered to be a self-contained collection of perhaps a few hundred families centred around a village or a hamlet. It is also highly likely that more than one overlapping community, communities with permeable boundaries and sub-communities, may exist. It is necessary to have a much more dynamic perception of community – a collection of conflicting interests, extending far beyond the village boundary (Jones and Wiggle, 1987).

The state

Historically, the provinces in South Africa had no tourism authority and, consequently, no provincial tourism institutional structures. South Africa's new constitution assigns responsibility for tourism development to the provinces. The 1996 White Paper on tourism provides a broad policy framework for the development of tourism in the country. While guided by national policy, it is important to note that in KwaZulu Natal the approach to tourism development must take into account the special features and circumstances of the province. The following state or parastatal institutions are responsible for the development of tourism in the province: The Department of Economic Affairs and Tourism, The KwaZulu Natal Nature Conservation Services (abbreviated to Conservation Services), and Tourism KwaZulu Natal.

The Department of Economic Affairs and Tourism is responsible for setting tourism policy and the necessary framework for tourism development in the province. Its responsibilities include drafting the necessary legislation, creating the basic infrastructure, creating institutional frameworks, and the promotion and development of tourism, particularly among previously disadvantaged communities.

It is the responsibility of the government to create a stable environment for investment, secure land tenure and an enabling environment for public-private partnerships. Key to this is the initiative known as the Lubombo Spatial Development Initiative (SDI). The Lubombo SDI is a programme of strategic initiatives aimed at unlocking and developing the inherent tourism potential of the region. There is an emphasis on the state as the promoter rather than the provider of services, creating the enabling environment and legislative framework for CBT to take place, while others can provide services. The key initiatives that constitute the basis of the framework include:

▶ proposed infrastructure development projects;

▶ the establishment of tourism clusters and anchor projects (and how these will affect the local economy through spin-offs);

▶ opportunities for cross-border tourism development with Mozambique and Swaziland;

- plans for local economic development through capacity building and small, medium and micro enterprise (SMME) development projects.

The SDI programme is based on the hypothesis that the crowding of private and public sector investment into specific spatial locations is a sound and sustainable means of achieving long-term economic development and restructuring ownership patterns in the South African economy (de Beer and Elliffe, 1997). SDI seeks to provide a favourable environment for all levels of government and the private sector to initiate development projects in the manufacturing, mining, tourism and agricultural sectors. As these new economic opportunities materialize, the lives of local inhabitants who now live in conditions of serious deprivation may be improved through sustained economic growth, long-term and sustainable employment creation, SMME development and local community empowerment. The Lubombo SDI has a tremendous opportunity for an integrated cultural and nature tourism experience, as well as providing local economic development.

KwaZulu Natal Nature Conservation Services

The KwaZulu Natal Nature Conservation Services (Conservation Services) is a parastatal authority established to manage conservation in the entire province. It was established recently as a result of the amalgamation of the previous Natal Parks Board and the former KwaZulu Bureau of Natural Resources. To enable the Conservation Services to develop tourism into a commercially viable business, key strategies have been adopted: the establishment of community conservation areas and the establishment of a trust company responsible for commercial tourism operations.

Community Conservation Areas

A community conservation area can be described as an area of land set aside by the tribal authority in its ward for the purpose of pursuing conservation in accordance with approved conservation policies as practised in KwaZulu Natal. It is an area of land of undetermined size which has been recognized as having a particular conservation and/or historical value for the tribal community it serves.

The Conservation Services encourages tribal authorities to set aside land for conservation. It believes its overall conservation strategy will be enhanced by:

- directly involving rural communities, particularly local authorities, in conservation management and all aspects of tourism;

- using these areas for environmental education for the local communities they serve, through a process of conservation by demonstration;
- providing jobs and job-related training directly related to conservation;
- providing habitat and space where wildlife can be stocked and/or where tourism can be developed;
- providing financial benefits to the tribal authorities and the adjacent communities.

Community conservation areas (CCA) are managed by a joint committee consisting of members of the tribal authority and representatives from the conservation services. The committee is chaired by a local *Inkosi* (chief) or his representative. This joint committee is responsible for formulating a management plan to govern the development and the administration of the area. Initially, the Conservation Services plays an active part in the development of a CCA through its membership with the joint management committee. This is very necessary as the CCA concept is new and the tribal authorities will need direct input from Conservation Services staff, expertise and funds, until the area is developed and running on its own. Once the CCA is operational, the Conservation Services then revert to the role of advisors through membership on the joint management committee. The joint management committee will determine the CCA's management strategy in terms of the management plan, and is empowered to enter into partnership agreements with other stakeholders in the development of tourism in the area (Department of Nature Conservation, 1997).

The Trust Company

A trust company has been put in place to advise the Conservation Services on its commercial activities. This trust company, with its own board of directors, is known as Isivuno (the Zulu word which means "to harvest"). Isivuno was established as the new commercial arm of the Conservation Services. Its role is to facilitate the formation of joint venture companies between the local community, private developers and the Conservation Services. The financial benefits generated will be redistributed to either tourism development or approved projects which will benefit conservation and local communities (Department of Nature Conservation, 1994).

Tourism KwaZulu Natal

Tourism KwaZulu Natal is a statutory body established to promote and market tourism in the province. It is governed by a board which has representatives from provincial government, local government, the tourism industry and labour. It also serves to coordinate and rationalize the activities of a multiplicity of local-level tourism marketing organizations.

The private sector

Communities do not have the institutional or the financial capacity to undertake ecotourism projects on their own. Private sector involvement in community based tourism projects is essential. The private sector must be encouraged to involve itself in tourism development as operators, suppliers of services, developers or financiers. Private sector developers possess sound business acumen and access to capital. Their business drive, combined with the Conservation Services' ecological and conservation expertise and the community's resources, will optimize the balance between wise land use and economical development of resources.

Non-governmental organizations

Non-governmental organizations working in the fields of conservation and development can play a significant role in facilitating the development of community based tourism. A large measure of support must be given to those who lack economic and political power against local and outside vested interests — not in the patronizing sense of "speaking for them but giv[ing] them the means to speak for themselves" (Jones and Wiggle, 1987, p. 108). NGOs are seen as more neutral than government officials and therefore have the capacity to induce trust among members of a community. They are less subject to political controls and intervention. NGOs could provide a range of support services which include capacity and institutional building, bringing stakeholders together, arbitration for conflict resolution, access to funding, and the facilitation of negotiations between local communities, the private sector and government.

PARTNERSHIP MODELS FOR THE DEVELOPMENT OF TOURISM FACILITIES

Various models designed to facilitate local participation in tourism projects in South Africa have been proposed (de Beer and Elliffe, 1997). These vary significantly among communities according to local conditions, needs and interests.

A partnership agreement between the community and one or more of the other stakeholders may often be more suitable than a community attempting to do everything entirely with its own human, physical and financial resources. The models presented below draw on the work of de Beer and Elliffe (1997) in which they propose a number of conceptual models for promoting local participation in tourism development projects.

Community owned venture

In this model, the community can own and develop all infrastructure services and facilities relating to tourism development. They would be responsible for mobilizing the necessary capital and expertise to plan, construct, operate and maintain the necessary infrastructure, facilities and services, as well as be responsible for environmental management. This model, though potentially very empowering, would in the short-term constitute an extremely high risk for the community because they may lack the institutional capacity to apply it.

A partnership between the community and the state

The second alternative represents a partnership between the community and the state. In this case, the state would manage tourism, the environment and small, medium and micro enterprise (SMME) development and support functions, on behalf of the community. The state then assumes, on an agency/management contract basis, responsibility for the operation and maintenance of infrastructure and facilities, environmental management and regulatory functions, SMME development and support and the mobilizing of needed funding. According to the terms of this model, the community would receive profits minus the costs associated with the role played by the state.

Lease agreement between the community and the private sector

In the third model, the private sector is mobilized by a lease agreement or a management contract to operate facilities that have been developed by the community on communal land. The community is responsible for building and maintaining the infrastructure, including mobilizing the necessary funds. The private sector is responsible for environmental management and for facilitating SMME development and support. Two options exist for benefits that flow to the community. If there is a lease agreement, a lease fee would be paid to the community on a regular basis. In the case of a management contract, all returns minus costs would be paid to the community.

Joint venture between community and private sector

In the fourth model, the community enters into a partnership with the private sector to develop the tourism potential of the area. The private developer would be responsible for developing, operating and maintaining all tourism infrastructure and facilities, environmental management, as well as SMME development and support functions. The advantage of this model is it offsets some of the constraints facing the community. These include obtaining the necessary financing and addressing the need for institutional capacity to perform environmental management and SMME development and support functions. The benefits that flow to the community include short-term concession fee payments based on a percentage of turnover. It also offers the community a genuine equity share in the operations.

The long-term vision in this scenario should be to transfer all existing ecotourism facilities into joint venture partnerships with the local community and private sector, where feasible. This would then make it possible to tap the marketing and business acumen of the private sector, reduce revenue leakages from regions where protected areas contribute to socio-economic management, stimulate private sector involvement in rural areas, create jobs, support equity holding and entrepreneurial opportunities associated with tourism, and create a sense of ownership and accountability among local communities for the environment.

When entering into a partnership, it is necessary to ask who represents the community. A mechanism is needed to represent the community's interests in terms of equity share in the management and decision-making of various operations, as well as in terms of the distribution of benefits flowing to the community. It is proposed that a community trust be elected to represent the community.

The community will elect a board of directors (every three to five years) and the BOD will appoint a permanent management committee to be responsible for the following key functions: membership of the community trust, allocation of benefits that flow from community enterprises, identification and prioritization of community projects, interaction with the private sector, interaction with the state and capacity building.

TOURISM ACTIVITIES

Community based tourism offers unique opportunities for including previously neglected communities in tourism's business activities. Opportunities for involvement include ownership of the tourist facilities by the community through shared equity, management and associated employment opportunities (for example, taxi drivers, tavern owners, tour operators, marketers, trainers, booking agents, laundry workers, curio and crafts sellers, construction workers, vegetable producers, charcoal production entrepreneurs, etc.).

Local people often possess immense natural and cultural knowledge of their local environment. With some basic training, they can become efficient tour guides. At Kosi Bay in the KwaDapha area of Maputaland, an NGO-sponsored community resource optimization programme (CROP) helps local communities run a rustic tented camp – the first camp owned and run purely by local communities. This venture is helping local communities reap the benefits of a growing interest in the fascinating life cycle of turtles which nest along the Maputaland coast. Members of the community were constantly being approached by tourists eager to witness the turtles' legendary nesting behaviour. A few community members saw an opportunity to exploit their knowledge and make some money in the growing tourism industry. After an initial training period, the Conservation Services allowed four guides to operate their own successful turtle tours on the beaches near Kosi Bay (African Wildlife, 1997). CBT policies can do much to encourage local entrepreneurship and they enable a greater percentage of tourism revenue to be retained within the local economy (Ceballos-Lascurain, 1996).

Support Services

Viewing the community as competent and resourceful implies an assumption that they have access to information and resources which enable them to make informed decisions. This is not always the case. Initially, due to a lack of experience, the community will not be competent to undertake most of the tasks required of it. Community based tourism will never be sustainable without adequate support services. It is the task of all the stakeholders to see to it that such services are put into place. Areas that need special attention are training, capacity building, business skills, access to finance, negotiating skills, marketing, natural resource management, and monitoring and evaluation of the tourism projects.

IMPACTS

Even the most conscientious tourism venture can introduce new pressures into a local ecosystem and have an impact on local culture. Impacts may be classified into environmental, social and economic. To determine the optimal level of tourism development for a specific destination area, all of these must be considered. Some of the more important impacts are outlined below.

Environmental

Overcrowding, the misuse of natural resources, the construction of buildings and infrastructure, as well as other activities associated with tourism, affect the environment. In general, the impacts of tourism vary according to the number and nature of tourists and the characteristics of the site. The individual tourist normally has relatively little impact. Problems arise, however, if there are large numbers of tourists or the resource is overused. Thus, while tourism can be a lucrative source of revenue for a protected area, it can also present a major management problem. The negative impacts of tourism development can only be managed effectively if they have been identified, measured and evaluated.

Social

Socio-cultural impacts are the outcome of particular kinds of social relationships that occur between tourists and hosts as a result of contact. Often, the socio-cultural impacts of tourism on the local or host population are neglected, but they must be carefully monitored if tourism is to be considered a truly renewable resource.

A history of removal and restriction on communal use of natural resources in areas declared as conservation lands has led to resistance on the part of some residents. Social impact assessment will be necessary in some areas to ascertain how various factions within communities are likely to be affected by, and respond to, tourism development so that mitigating measures can be properly planned.

Economic

To assess economic impact the following questions need to be asked:
1. How do financial benefits reach the community? e.g. direct payments to the community in the form of rent, gate fees, profit share.

2. To what extent are earnings, wages or shared community income, distributed across the community?

3. How successful have these projects been in creating employment?

4. To what extent has tourism development encouraged the creation of secondary income generating activities? e.g. laundry services, charcoal making, transport, etc.

Carrying capacity is a useful concept which measures impact. Environmental carrying capacity may be defined as the capacity of an ecosystem to support healthy organisms while maintaining its productivity, adaptability, and capability of renewal. In other words, carrying capacity represents a threshold level of human activity – if exceeded, the resource base will deteriorate (Wolters, 1991). Tourism carrying capacity specifically refers to the carrying capacity of the biophysical and social environment with respect to tourist activity and development (*ibid.*, 1991). It represents the maximum level of visitor use and related infrastructure that an area can accommodate. If this is exceeded, deterioration of the areas' resources, diminished visitor satisfaction and/or adverse impacts on society, economy and culture of the area can be expected to ensue (McIntyre and Hetherington, 1991).

Although the concept of tourism carrying capacity is not very difficult to comprehend in theory, it is difficult to quantify empirically, as there is no single definition to apply for tourism or for the environment. It is commonly recognized that there are no fixed or standard tourism carrying capacity values. Rather, carrying capacity is contingent upon place, season and time, user behaviour, facility design, patterns and levels of management, and the dynamic character of the environments themselves. Moreover, it is not always possible to separate measurements of tourist activity from other human activities. Nevertheless, community based tourism planning can benefit from the attempt to define tourism carrying capacity for a specific site or sites, as this will offer an indication of the limits and limitations of tourism development.

BANZI PAN SAFARI LODGE: CASE STUDY

The Banzi Pan Safari Lodge, a joint venture between a local community, the Conservation Services and the private developer Wilderness Safaris, is an example of a CBT project in the province. Situated in the Maputaland region of KwaZulu Natal, just south of the Mozambique border, the camp is built on the edge of the Banzi Pan on the Ndumo floodplain system. Ndumo is considered to be the finest birdwatching locale in South Africa, where over 400 species (60%) of South Africa's birds have been recorded. It offers tented accommodation on raised wooden decks linked by a tree canopy walkway several metres above the ground.

To develop this project, the Conservation Services, represented by the commercial arm Isivuno, facilitated the formation of a development company and an operating company in partnership with the host community, the Mathenjwa Tribe, and a private tour operator. The Banzi Pan Safari Lodge required an initial capital start up of R2.5 million. The Conservation Services provided R1.05 million in equity and the balance went into a shareholder's loan to make up a total of 58% equity holding in the development company. The remaining 42% was taken up by the KwaZulu Finance Corporation, a parastatal which loans capital to businesses.

The Mathenjwa Tribal Authority was invited to take up 25% of the Conservation Services' shares in the development company. The Conservation Services is currently holding these shares in trust until the Mathenjwa Tribal Authority empowers the already constituted Mathenjwa Tourism and Development Association to act on its behalf.

The development company, Banzi (Pty) Ltd., has leased the tourism facilities to an operating company which has engaged Wilderness Safaris, a private tour operator, to manage the day-to-day operation of the lodge. Wilderness Safaris has acquired a 50% share of the operating company. The remaining 50% is owned by the KZNCS and local community at 37.5% and 12.5% respectively (Department of Nature Conservation, 1994). The community derives benefits from a variety of cash flows, including a proportional percentage of land rentals, 4% of turnover, profit sharing from both the development and operating companies and 25% of the gate fees.

This project demonstrates how the community can get involved in tourism projects, with shared equity and decision-making responsibilities in the operating company. Not only do host communities share in the benefits of the development, but as business partners they share in joint decision-making, planning and accepting responsibility for tourism development.

CONCLUSION

South Africa's transition to democracy brought with it new opportunities to include the previously neglected majority of people in the benefits of conservation and tourism activities. Community based tourism is increasingly being adopted by national and provincial governments as a mechanism to promote socio-economic development, encourage the sustainable use of the natural resource base and involve people in the process of their own development. However, for community based tourism to realize its full potential, a well planned strategy needs to be put into place so that tourism development can take place within a guiding development framework. This proposed conceptual framework for community based tourism in the province of KwaZulu Natal, South Africa, may, with a few changes, be applied to other areas as well. It attempts to clarify some of the conceptual issues, identify the major stakeholders and their roles and responsibilities. It broadly acknowledges that the relationship between the community, state, private sector and NGOs is intrinsically intertwined and provides the basis for adopting a more integrated approach to the development of community based tourism projects.

REFERENCES

African Wildlife. 1997: Turtle Power. *African Wildlife*, 51 (3) May/June, 24-27.

Ceballos-Lascurain, H. 1996: *Tourism, Ecotourism, and Protected Areas.* Gland: IUCN.

Cernea, M. 1991: *Putting People First: Sociological Variables in Rural Development, 2nd. ed.* New York: Oxford University Press.

Culpan, R. 1987: International Tourism Model for Developing Countries. *Annals of Tourism Research,* 6 (1), 36-48.

de Beer, G. and Elliffe, S. 1997: *Tourism Development and the Empowerment of Local Communities.* Johannesburg: Development Bank of South Africa.

Department of Nature Conservation. 1994: *A Policy of Sharing: a Case Study of Private Sector and Host Community Involvement in Ecotourism Development of Protected Areas.* Eshowe: Department of Nature Conservation.

Department of Nature Conservation. 1997: *Community Conservation Areas: Draft Document.* Eshowe: Department of Nature Conservation.

Handley, G. 1996: Can Ecotourism Save South Africa. *Enterprise,* 103 October, 137-139.

Jones, B.T.B. 1996: *Institutional Relationships, Capacity and Sustainability.* Windhoek: Directorate of Environmental Affairs, Ministry of Tourism.

Jones, J. and Wiggle, I. 1987: The Concept and Politics of Integrated Community Development. *Community Development Journal,* 22 (2), 107-122.

McIntyre, G. and Hetherington, A. 1991: *Sustainable Tourism Development: Guidelines for Local Planners.* Madrid: World Tourism Organisation.

Pimbert, M.P. and Pretty, J.N. 1997: Parks, People and Professionals: Putting 'Participation' into Protected Area Management. In B.G. Krishna and M.P. Pimpert (eds.), *Social Change and Conservation.* London: Earthscan.

Pretty, J. 1995: The Many Interpretations of Participation. *Focus,* 16 (1), 4-5.

Taylor, M. 1996: *Community Based Natural Resource Management: A Select Foundation Bibliography with Emphasis on Southern Africa.* Harare: Africa Resources Trust.

Wolters, T.M. 1991: *Tourism Carrying Capacity.* Madrid: World Tourism Organisation.

World Bank. 1995: *South Africa: Natural Resource Issues in Environmental Policy.* Washington D.C.: The World Bank.

Chapter 4

Tourism, Bio-diversity and Community Development in Kenya

by Donald G. Reid, Isaac Sindiga, Nadine Evans and Stephen Ongaro

Introduction

This chapter reports on a study in Kenya which addresses tourism's potential as a force for enhancing the environment while improving the local standard of living and contributing to national economies. Tourism, and particularly ecotourism, is regarded by many developing countries as an instrument for addressing their current and pressing problems. Primary among these problems are declining economies, resource depletion and degrading environments. As governments exploit their tourism potential, they have come to realize that the involvement of local people and communities is vital if tourism is to become part of the solution to these problems and not an additional negative outcome. Inherent in this realization is the fact that environmental protection and community development and individual welfare are intricately linked and cannot be planned separately, as has often been the case. Additionally, each of these goals must have equal focus – one cannot be placed in a subordinate position as the means to achieving the other.

Tourism around the globe, and particularly in the developing world, suffers from uneven development, ensuring erratic returns and disproportionate incomes. This is particularly noticeable when examining the local level. Local communities are often the front line in service provision but last in line when it comes to the benefits of development. Individuals in communities with a unique cultural tradition are also often part of the attraction themselves, whether they want to be or not. These inequities and intrusions are a consequence of poor planning or poorly managed tourism destinations. While individual businesses and business people are well prepared and educated to capitalize on the tourism experience, the community is often last to organize itself for development and subsequent benefits. More often than not, communities initially fail to realize the value to the tourist of the environment in which they live, and only become aware after an outside organization or company has exploited the destination or attraction and profited handsomely from it.

This situation is particularly evident in Kenya and other African countries. Many large-scale organizations, be they national government institutions or transnational companies, develop areas as tourist destinations, but exclude local communities from the planning and development of those areas. Then, as tourists pour into the area, the resource base on which the local traditional economies have depended for their meager survival is often overtaxed. What begins as resource sharing becomes a competition with the "success" of tourism development. Governments initially create national parks and reserves to protect wildlife. However, to generate enough revenue to survive and compete in the globalized economy, the park resources are exploited beyond their capacity.

In Kenya, many national parks have been created and are managed by the Kenya Wildlife Service (KWS) for the purpose of protecting the bio-diversity of the country's natural resources. While this policy can be seen as noble, it has often produced conflict and hardship for local people who have had to adjust their traditional living patterns to accommodate this national initiative. The Kenya situation is another example of national goals conflicting with, and impacting on, local lifestyles.

Much of this conflict can be avoided if the community is actively involved in whatever plans are developed for their area and shares in the benefits. Improved tourism policies could alleviate poverty by fueling economic growth and providing for equitable resource distribution. Community participation in tourism development in poor rural areas such as Kenya's Maasailand has the potential to empower the local people by increasing incomes and employment and developing skills and institutions (Ashley and Garland, 1994). "Above all, community participation could guarantee local support for conservation and sustainable natural resource use (and a sustainable tourism product)" (ibid., p.2). Only when rural communities are involved in wildlife control and management do conflicts and competition for resources, which threaten parks, become minimized (Ashley, 1995).

When protected areas were established in Kenya, as elsewhere in Africa, indigenous communities were frequently displaced from their ancestral lands. The British wanted to create islands of undisturbed environment approximating their natural state. Local people were moved out of protected areas and denied any share of park revenues (Talbot and Olindo, 1990). This policy was later relaxed to allow for some land uses such as fuel wood collection, herding, etc. and the sharing of revenues from national reserves. However, these activities were not allowed in national parks such as Amboseli. As a result, the Maasai clashed with the authorities over range resources. "To vent their anger, the Maasai started to spear wild animals" (Talbot and Olindo, 1990, p. 70), causing great concern among the authorities.

Although the government subsequently conceded to some form of revenue sharing from the Amboseli gate fees, the situation remained unsatisfactory. This led the local Maasai community to form wildlife associations intended to organize community participation in order to derive direct benefits from tourism.

Recently, the KWS has recognized that if the original goal of bio-diversity preservation is to be achieved, the needs of people involved must be met. Unless the people residing in the area begin to see that tourism directly benefits them personally and collectively, they are not likely to cooperate with the KWS/government policies. They will continue to use the local resources to their benefit – in this case herding and farming, which are in direct competition with wildlife preservation. To move closer to the reality of community involvement in planning and development of national parks and tourism, the KWS has reorganized itself into three divisions: bio-diversity, tourism and partnership.

The partnership division is commissioned to bring the stakeholders in national park development into the planning and development process. This study examines the philosophy and goals of this policy and its impact after implementation. Moreover, the study intends to determine what components warrant incorporation into a general model which can be used by other organizations facing similar issues and conflicts between land use for developing tourism and maintaining the affected indigenous peoples' culture and lifestyle.

This study is an attempt to investigate the intricate problems and barriers which limit the true participation of local communities in the development and resulting benefits of Kenya's tourism development. Additionally, the research attempts to provide a conceptual framework for development which overcomes these barriers and places the community at the centre of the initiative. To achieve this overall goal, a number of objectives were developed to guide the study. They were:

- to document Kenya's traditional tourism development and planning process which speaks directly to community involvement;
- to develop an appreciation for the social, cultural and environmental impacts of the present tourist attraction and system in the area;
- to investigate in a macro sense, the benefits and costs of tourism and ecotourism systems to the Maasai communities.

STUDY AREA

This study focused on the Amboseli region of Kenya. The area contains one of Kenya's most notable national parks in the midst of the Maasai, a traditional semi-nomadic group of people. The Maasai live on seven group ranches which surround the park. They share the resources of the area with wildlife and, now, with tourists.

The Amboseli National Park is situated approximately 240 km to the southeast of Nairobi, the country's capital. The park lies at the northern foot of Mount Kilimanjaro which enhances the background of the park and is an additional tourism attraction for the area (Figure 4.1).

Figure 4.1 Study Area

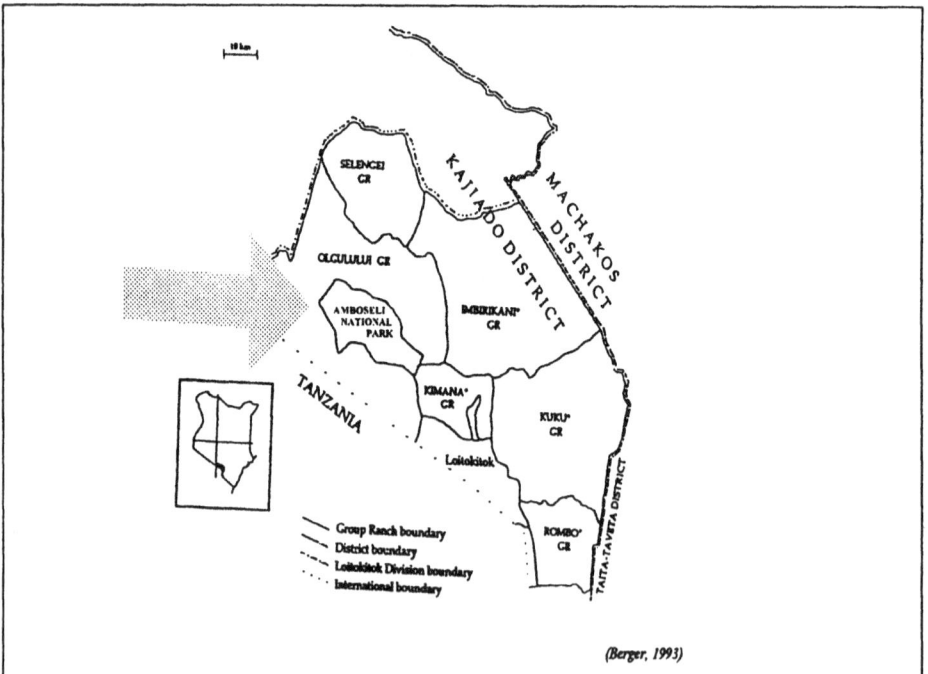

(Berger, 1993)

62

The present Amboseli National Park is a remnant of the Southern Game Reserve established in 1906 which occupied an area of 27,700 km^2. The Southern Game Reserve was reduced to an area of 3260 km^2 in 1948 and renamed Amboseli National Reserve. It was administered by the National Park Trustees. In 1961, Amboseli became a County Council game reserve administered by the Kajiado County Council.

The government realized that Amboseli possessed unique ecological values which required proper management. A 1971 presidential decree declared that an area of 390 km^2 be set aside for wildlife conservation and tourism. The boundaries of the park were established in 1972 and the site gazetted as government land. The Kenya Wildlife Service was established in 1989 and became responsible for the management of all national parks in the country. However, the Ol Tukai area of Amboseli National Park, a wetland with backwaters and streams, remains as an enclave which is the property of the Kajaido County Council.

Amboseli National Park is located in Kajiado District of the Rift Valley Province. Administratively, the district is divided into three divisions: Kajiado, Loitokitok and Ngong. Loitokitok division, which is situated at the southern end of Kajiado District, is the administrative unit covering the Amboseli ecosystem. A district officer is based in Loitokitok who administers the division with the help of chiefs and sub-chiefs at locational and sub-locational levels. The local government authority for the area is the Kajaido County Council.

The people indigenous to the Amboseli ecosystem are the Maasai who have traditionally lived as semi-nomadic subsistence pastoralists. They do not eat game meat except during severe drought when elands and buffaloes, considered close relatives of cows, may be consumed. Their subsistence pastoralism and cultural dietary taboos have preserved large wildlife populations within the Amboseli ecosystem.

The Amboseli region is believed to have been a lake in the past. It is dotted with several swamps which are fed by subterranean springs originating from Mt. Kilimanjaro. These swamps are the Amboseli region's principle water sources. Wildlife congregate there during the dry season and disperse into the surrounding areas soon after the wet season grass sprouts.

The area receives little rainfall. It is common for the local pastoralists to constantly move about with their livestock in search of pasture and water. The seasonal movement of the Maasai and their herds always coincides with the movement of wildlife within the Amboseli ecosystem. Wet season movement is always away from the swamps. However, when the water becomes scarce during the dry season, movement of both pastoralists and wildlife is towards the Tukai swamps.

In 1977, the Maasai were asked to stop taking their livestock into the Amboseli park. In return, they were promised water pumped from one of the swamps into tanks situated outside the park. This marked the end of the Maasai people's freedom of access to the water and pasture resources of the Amboseli National Park.

Most of the land around the park has been sub-divided to create group ranches: Olgulului, Olgulului/Ololorashi, Eselengei, Mbirikani, Kuku, Rombo, and Kimana. The establishment of group ranches did not take into consideration the wet and dry seasons or the grazing patterns of the local people's herds. The Maasai view pastureland and water as communal rather than private property; grazing is not confined to one's group ranch but rather the entire region. Indeed, the expansive grassland of the Embakasi and Athi-kapiti plains around Nairobi occasionally host the Maasai herdsman.

Crop farming appears to be gaining popularity in Loitokitok division, especially in the highlands towards the Kilimanjaro, Kuku and Kimana group ranches. Farming is spreading in the area and mostly involves people from other Kenyan communities. The farming area most affected by the parks ecosystem appears to be Kimana with its large swamp and the Tikondo River. Irrigation water from the Nolturesh springs supports agricultural activities in Kuku "B" group ranch. The main crops grown are beans, onions and maize. There is extensive agricultural activity in the highlands area between Loitokitok town and the Kenya/Tanzania boundary.

Competition for pasture and water seems to be the central conflict between the local communities and the wildlife. It is estimated that over 80% of the wild animals within the Amboseli ecosystem are found on the group ranches outside the park boundaries. Wild animals come to share the resources with livestock on group ranches. Occasionally, predators prey on domestic animals, herbivores destroy crops and people are injured or even killed by wild animals.

Wildlife is also responsible for the spread of diseases such as East Coast Fever and the Malignant Cattarrh Fever. The use of cattle dips is not effective because wild animals do not receive the same treatment.

The Amboseli National Park and group ranches are the focus of tourism-related economic activities. Direct revenue is earned as gate fee payments by visitors to the park and Kimana wildlife sanctuary. KWS has leased land to the Amboseli Serena Lodge while the Kajiado County Council has leased land to Kilimanjaro Safari Club, Amboseli Lodge and the Ol Tukai Lodge at the Ol Tukai enclave. Kimana group ranch has leased land to Kimana Lodge. There is also a tented camp within Kimana Sanctuary, the Leopard Tented Camp. Imbirikani group ranch has a private tented campsite near Chyulu Hills. There is great potential for the establishment of Maasai traditional villages or cultural *manyattas* to sell culture and artifacts to tourists.

STUDY METHODOLOGY

Several methods were employed in this research. The nature of the project – to determine the intent and extent to which community development initiatives are represented by the KWS and the stakeholders in the tourism enterprise – demanded a qualitative research approach. Qualitative research answers questions of meaning, while quantitative data collection and analysis focuses on issues of how many and how much. The quantitative approach to research is usually interested in making inferences about a population from a sample. This was not the intent of the research discussed here. This project attempted to document the successes and failures of an initiative of a national tourism agency (in this case the KWS) which is working to involve the various communities and stakeholders in the planning process in order to widen the sense of ownership, stewardship and protection of the natural resources in and around the national parks. As a consequence of the intent of this study, the research protocol consisted mainly of interviews, participant observation, the analysis of official government policy and planning documents, and NGO strategy statements.

Phase one

Field work began with several days of visiting the International Development Research Centre's (IDRC) office and library in Nairobi. There, general documents, such as the Kenya Eighth National Development Plan (Republic of Kenya, 1997), were reviewed as an orientation to Kenya and the impending work. Meetings were held with IDRC officers, particularly those involved in tourism research, to determine the scope and range of previous and continuing studies.

This phase continued with the research team meeting at the Kisii Campus of Egerton University. One week was spent in orientation and preparation for the site visits to the KWS headquarters in Nairobi and the communities in and around the Amboseli region. During this orientation period, interview guides were developed and a list of key informants to be interviewed was prepared. Strategies for on-the-ground field work were set so that maximum benefit could be achieved in the short period of time available for data collection in the field.

Phase two

The second phase of the research was conducted in Nairobi and mainly centered at the KWS headquarters. The purpose was twofold: to search out and analyze pertinent documents where possible and to interview key KWS personnel for their insights on the partnership development and tourism aspects of their strategy. A small number of Kenyan NGO executive directors based at the KWS headquarters were also interviewed.

Additionally, the research team attended a workshop with the KWS partnership division and a large number of the stakeholders in the enterprise. Data pertinent to this research was recorded while the meeting was in progress. This meeting provided an opportunity to observe the interactions between the KWS and the stakeholder groups. The purpose of the workshop was to establish a yearly working agenda for this body and to outline the issues the group saw as priority for attention over the next year. While attendance at the workshop was not initially anticipated as part of the research protocol prior to contact with the KWS, it proved to be a very important activity of the research project.

Phase three

The third phase of the research was devoted to field work in communities adjacent to the Amboseli National Park. The purpose of this field work was to observe the implementation of the KWS partnership initiative which seeks to bring the local communities and other stakeholder groups into the decision-making process as a full partner. The KWS hopes that by making them full partners in the process, the bio-diversity objective of the KWS will be better served.

A field research station was established in Loitokitok near Amboseli National Park. From here, site visits to a number of the seven group ranches and park administration offices were made. Local officials, politicians, chairs of group ranches, KWS field personnel, hoteliers and the general public were interviewed. The research team also visited local Maasai communities to observe tourism's impact on the community first-hand. Interviews were conducted for the most part by two researchers, one to conduct the interview and the other to act as recorder. Journals were kept for constructing observational data.

The fieldwork portion of the study focused on the Amboseli National Park for a number of reasons:

1. There is evidence that the group ranches just outside the Amboseli National Park have become heavily degraded as a result of overgrazing (Talbot and Olindo, 1990). Amboseli is, therefore, an excellent field laboratory to test the hypothesis that community participation in wildlife-based tourism leads to resource regeneration and sustainability;

2. There are considerable studies on the Amboseli ecosystem which can be a benchmark against which contemporary change can be measured (for example, Berger, 1993; Western, 1982);

3. Amboseli is one of Kenya's leading tourist attractions, hosting over 100,000 visitors each year; and

4. The local Maasai community of Amboseli has organized itself to participate directly in tourism development. This study relies on observational data to appraise the performance of community involvement in tourism projects to date.

Phase four

Phase four of the project focused on a return to the analysis of documents found in the KWS library. Many NGOs such as the Kenya Ecotourism Association and the Kenya Association of Tour Operators were also interviewed during this phase. These first four phases of the research project were completed between late July and August of 1997.

Throughout the research project, a total of 27 key informants were interviewed, numerous participant observations were made (usually in Maasai communities), a focus group workshop with stakeholders was attended, and 44 documents were analyzed.

RESEARCH FINDINGS

Offering a section which summarizes the findings and conclusions of a research project is always the most challenging, but also the most rewarding task. In this case, it is doubly difficult because of the intricate nature of the culture of the group which constitutes the largest section of the study area.

Many Maasai still live a semi-nomadic lifestyle, travelling considerable distances to feed and water their cattle. Among the more traditional members of this culture, the accumulation of cattle still demonstrates wealth and status, and much effort is devoted to procuring and caring for these animals. Volumes have been written on the Maasai and their culture, so this chapter will not dwell on the subject further. Suffice it to say that traditional Maasai culture and the environment in which they live have the potential to be affected greatly by the introduction of the market economy as represented through tourism.

This research assumes that the goal of the KWS is to enhance the bio-diversity of the region, while increasing the income of local communities through expanding tourism activities at the community level. Given this premise, one must start with the culture of the group which has been targeted for development and determine the specific facilitators and inhibitors for that development in the unique case under study.

The authors of this study recognize the sensitive nature of this task. Culture is the method by which a people understand themselves and view their world. Following Goodenough's lead, Keesing and Keesing define culture as a "...system of shared ideas, to the conceptual designs that underlie the ways in which a people live. Culture, as defined, refers to what men [sic] learn, not what they do and make" (1971, p. 21). Introducing new realities, methods or artifacts into a culture can have drastic second order consequences to that culture. The literature is filled with such incidents.

Outsiders often view traditional cultures with some nostalgia and wish for its preservation. Some would argue that to introduce new technologies or economic methods into a traditional culture borders on cultural genocide. However, one also needs to remember that cultures are not static, but rather dynamic and change over time. The exercise needs to be one of assisting the Maasai to develop and grow as they wish and not to impose an alternate lifestyle on them.

This may be easier said than done. Many forces and competing interests are already at work in the study area, which will have a direct effect on the traditional patterns of the Maasai. The KWS has embarked on a commendable programme to restore to earlier levels the wildlife which have become threatened because of human pressures. In contrast, farmers are renting land from the Maasai to grow crops, further reducing available grazing lands for both wildlife and cattle. As animal populations increase, either wild or domestic, more pressure is placed on the existing resources to support those animals. Tourists visiting these areas, particularly those from developed countries, bring with them different behaviours and expectations, some of which are seen by the local people as desirable for themselves. Mass media such as television is also having the usual effect, as it does in other parts of the world. Even policies of the International Monetary Fund and other world economic organizations are contributing to massive change.

Because of these pressures, at some point, either in the near future or somewhat later, the Maasai may need to consider ways other than the accumulation of cattle as a basis for social organization. A basis which is more in harmony with the needs of the environment and the other economic development going on around them could help to solve some of their subsistence needs, as well as being of benefit to the environment. Moving to a money exchange economy may provide several advantages to help deal with some of the issues raised in this research. While some may see this as interference in a culture, others would argue that the Maasai culture will be severely exploited if they are not encouraged to adapt to what is already taking place around them.

It stands to reason, therefore, that the traditional culture of the Maasai is bound to change at a rapid pace, as it has for other traditional cultures in the recent past. One hopes, however, to assist with the transition so that change is beneficial to the local community and people and does not result in the ravishment of what should be rightfully theirs. Tourism has the potential to influence change in either direction. If handled properly, it could be of great benefit to the Maasai and other traditional societies faced with the same kind of change, or, alternately, it could provide the vehicle which destroys a very proud and flourishing culture, in addition to devastating the environment.

Education and training

Perhaps the most limiting element to the development of tourism, and hence the economy in the Amboseli area, is the lack of education among the local population. Almost all of those interviewed cited the lack of basic education as the key element to development and growth in the future.

General education at the primary level, and specific education with adults through focused job-related training, is badly needed at the community level. With adults, fundamental education such as reading and writing skills can be incorporated into job training programs. Skills like accounting, bookkeeping, budgeting, as well as learning about the culture of the visitors, could then be taught. However, most of these competencies are dependent on the basics of reading, writing and numeracy.

This education should also include an understanding of the tourist's needs. The tourist must be seen to be more than just a walking money machine. Some of the lodge and hotel managers interviewed were concerned with interaction between the Maasai and the tourist. Often tourists feel very uncomfortable with the deluge of hawkers descending on them when they stop to shop or just to rest. The interaction between the Maasai (mainly women) and tourists may, in fact, inhibit transactions.

Given the Maasai's general lack of education in the rural countryside, particularly in the Amboseli region, those who are educated occupy a relatively elevated status in the community. While this is understandable, it can lead to an isolated elite making decisions which don't always benefit the common people. Some of the interviewees emphasized the importance of adult education programs to deal with such issues.

Special attention must be given to girls who marry early and leave school before reaching a minimum standard, and to boys who leave school early to become *Moran* (warriors). The general attitudes which discourage education of females also need to be addressed. Often they are married off by their fathers before they have completed primary school. Some NGOs and the government have implemented programs to address this issue and in the future it can be expected that more young people, including females, will complete secondary school education.

However, most traditional Maasai are still semi-nomadic, travelling considerable distances to water and graze their cattle. Educational organizations need to consider the special features of semi-nomadic life. Schools need to be strategically placed to accommodate this lifestyle. In cases where this will not work, boarding schools should be considered at both the primary and secondary level.

Post-primary education seems to be a privilege reserved for the community's elite. This was a major concern expressed by many of those interviewed. Equal access to higher education needs to be more attainable by all. This may require more emphasis placed on primary education so that more students will continue studies at the secondary level. At any rate, a lot of extension education work should be done to sensitize the community to the virtues of education, especially for females.

Contributing to this difficulty, elders in the most traditional villages don't pay sufficient attention to the educated young people in their communities. Elders need to learn the value of educated people as a resource, regardless of their age. At present, the culture values discipline and hierarchy over education, often leading to the rejection of the opinions or contributions of younger members of the group, no matter how enlightened they may be.

Locally based training of people already involved in the tourism industry would be a very logical place to begin the education process. This is already done by some of the Amboseli lodges and could possibly be expanded to accommodate local community people. This could be an important role for the private sector which was sought by those attending the partners workshop at the KWS headquarters, as reported earlier in this chapter.

Study tours are a very useful method of educating people who are engaged in a specific business. Such tours are now starting to be seen in the Amboseli area, although they mainly focus on the elite of the community. This practice needs to be expanded to other sectors of the community, including primary school children and perhaps curio hawkers, in order to broaden their conception of tourism and of other cultures. Most Maasai have never had the experience of being a tourist themselves, so are unsure of how to interface with tourists who come to visit them. A better understanding and appreciation of the needs of the tourist should be high on the priority list for bridging this gap.

Many of the interview respondents suggested that seminars and workshops (mainly around management matters) are sporadic and need to be held more regularly and expanded to include a wider variety of subjects and learners. These types of educational opportunities could assist greatly with activities like curio sales, which need better organization and management. Additionally, hawking curios should be done through a co-operative system so that the tourists are not scared off by hordes of sellers. This would require more training of the local Maasai curio dealers. Many issues around the curio sales and the interaction between local cultures and visitors were of concern to several of the hotel managers who were interviewed. Some hotels and lodges are now making special arrangements with specific *Manyattas* (villages) to take their guests for a cultural experience. At the end of the visit, the trading of curios occurs in a more controlled and organized manner than otherwise ensues on the village streets.

A recent Maasai experiment has been the creation of the Kimana sanctuary and *Bomas*. This effort has been supported by the KWS and outside aid sources. The Kimana experiment incorporates employee training (wildlife scouts), as well as the development of infrastructure (lodges), while preserving wildlife as the attraction. It has not taken widespread advantage of cultural tourism, as yet, and needs to be more active on this front. While the initiative of the Kimana sanctuary and *Bomas* has not had time to prove its worth, it seems to be achieving the intended results and is a potential model which could be considered for implementation in other locations where the KWS is attempting to diversify tourism, and perhaps in other countries as well.

Competing interests

The many conflicts which plague everyday life are the major antagonisms which seem to be motivating the KWS and the communities to find new ways of conducting business. Generally, these conflicts arise because of the traditional/modern culture interface. Tourism is a modern economic activity, while the Maasai are deeply embedded in a traditional semi-nomadic herding economy. The traditional culture does not value the market economy except as a support to the traditional economy. However, the demands of both tourism and the tourist cannot be satisfied if it remains a part-time activity. Tourism must become more central if it is to reach its potential for improving the Maasai's material life and preserving their natural surroundings.

The root problem is essentially a human and community problem and should be addressed from that perspective. When priority is given to people and communities, the desired level of bio-diversity will result. As long as there is a desire on the part of the Maasai to increase the numbers of animals in the area, be they domestic or wild, there will be competition for resources to care for those animals. Until the life of the people is improved, and until that improvement is clearly connected to the development of tourism, this problem is sure to continue.

Water seems to be the largest issue for the community people interviewed. Water must be delivered to communities outside the park, otherwise the Maasai will continue to water and graze their cattle inside the park boundaries, competing with wildlife for resources. There should be a system of water holes both in the park and surrounding it, so that wild animals will not need to invade community bore holes in the dry months. The creation of more water access points is critical.

As a means to increase income, some Maasai land owners are now renting out large sections of their land to non-Maasai farmers. With their new wealth, the Maasai purchase more cattle, further straining the available natural feed and water resources and increasing competition with the wildlife. This, of course, is the downside of increasing the importance of the money economy in the area. This should be a short-term problem, however, as cattle become less and less the symbol of wealth for the Maasai.

Traditional Maasai culture has both a positive and negative effect on community and individual lifestyles. The traditional position of women is problematic. Unless women leave the community and move to another location, they have little chance of being involved in the decision-making process of the community or the family, simply by virtue of their traditional standing in the community. There are, however, some notable exceptions to this general concern.

On the other hand, the traditional culture is unique and deserves preservation. Cultures evolve, and the positive aspects of the Maasai culture need to be preserved while the culture adapts to the modern world. Because tourism will hasten this change, it should be planned by local people and not outsiders.

There is some interest in subdividing the group ranches into individual plots. If this is done, it may accelerate the modernization of the traditional culture – and could have severe implications for wildlife transportation corridors, particularly between the Amboseli and Tsavo West National Parks. This plan should be considered very carefully before it is implemented.

There are problems with regard to compensation for animal damage. The interests and process of compensation, and the basis on which that process operates are not transparent. What will be compensated is not always known. Loss of human life and cattle appear to be compensated while damaged crops are not.

Perhaps even more confusing, especially to the Maasai themselves, is the formula for revenue sharing. This system seems to be complicated and little understood. It would appear that the revenue system is national rather than regional or local. The revenue from profitable parks is shared with communities adjacent to all the other parks in the country. Even after the regional allocation is determined, the KWS asks the group ranches in each area to decide how much each ranch should receive. This, of course, has led to a gridlock and revenue sharing has happened at a slow pace.

On the cultural tourism front, visits to cultural *Bomas* (villages) are not as accessible as desired. Tourists must make arrangements with the community administration before they are admitted, which limits spontaneous visits. Again, this may be a result of tourism being seen as a secondary activity, rather than as central to the communities. Or the problem may be that the cultural *Bomas* are also the residents' permanent living quarters. Cultural *Bomas* expressly set up to meet the needs of tourism would separate these functions, making tourist visits less intrusive. The Maasai need to understand that they are not just selling curios, but the understanding of their culture as well. This aspect of the business needs to be presented to the Maasai jointly by the tourism and partnership sections of the KWS.

Training of KWS in community development work (partnership)
Most of those interviewed felt the KWS has developed worthwhile policies regarding partnership in tourism development with the Maasai and other groups, but can find little evidence of widespread strategic implementation. All believe the idea of partnership is important and could lead to some important improvements in bio-diversity and the living standards of local people, but there is considerable scepticism with regard to implementation of this very worthwhile venture.

There is little evidence that those in charge of implementing the partnership program have formal or informal training in the area of group work, group dynamics, consulting or facilitation skills, or community development practice. If the KWS intends to continue leadership in this important initiative, it will need to bolster skill levels.

The KWS tourism staff also need training around product development and refinement. The regional tourism officer should have the mandate for training both community members and park staff with regard to tourism product development at the local level.

NGOs do not seem to be working in tourism in the field. The major exception to this is the COBRA project funded by USAID which is producing good results as demonstrated by Kimana. More NGO development in this area could help the KWS implement many of the needed training programs at both the national park and local level.

The KWS Wildlife Training Institute at Naivasha could expand its mandate and programs to include training in tourism-related areas for both KWS staff and local community people. People who are involved in tourism and are respected in their community should be the focus of this training, as they in turn are likely candidates for training others at the local level and in their own environment.

The development of a tourism development plan

At present, the KWS planning is basically an in-house affair. The KWS has a planning unit with a corporate planner and staff. The department heads and the corporate planner set the planning guidelines and budget indicators before launching the process. Proposed activities and budgets are generated at the regional level and presented to the department director who then refines them according to corporate needs and priorities. Plans are then submitted to the corporate planning department for final approval. Traditionally, these plans have focused on the wildlife and activities in the park. However, that may be changing in the future to include more emphasis on the areas adjacent to the park.

While the policy documents of the government (Republic of Kenya, 1997) and of the KWS (KWS, 1996) clearly indicate that the KWS wants to act in partnership with the local stakeholders, this policy does not yet have an implementation plan of action.

Strategic plans which outline the intent, role and function of the various partners are being developed. This task has been assigned to the group ranches themselves, as it should be. While this bottom-up approach may take longer, the group ranches' plans should see stronger local support than would plans outlined by the KWS itself. If this is to be a true partnership, the implementation design is best left to those who will be most affected by their development.

A Proposed Framework for Community Based Tourism Development

General considerations

While the KWS' primary focus on bio-diversity is most worthwhile, it must be balanced by equal emphasis on community development – by the KWS or another strong agency. Until community development gets equal attention, attempts to create greater bio-diversity are likely to stagnate.

Tourism becomes the means to achieving both goals. By working towards both ends, people will come to realize the local flora and fauna are important to their welfare and be much committed to their preservation. If all the attention is focused on preserving natural resources and enhancing bio-diversity, people understandably feel secondary to the animals of the park and the surrounding area. In our view, true partnership will come about only when the people of the area are convinced there is a focus on their well-being and they are not simply preservers of the wildlife for the benefit of tourism.

The KWS has started something immensely important by adopting the partnership project in its mandate. It is our view that the KWS is on the right track as it includes community development in its efforts towards sustainable increases in bio-diversity.

The mandate of the KWS, however, will not allow for community development to be given the same importance as bio-diversity. It is necessary, therefore, for some other organization to undertake this task. However, there does not appear to be another organization with adequate staff or funds to undertake such a large initiative.

Without community development, the whole project could be for nought. Those living at the local level will need to see dramatic increases in their standard of living if they are to become willing and enthusiastic participants in the KWS mandate. They must come to the conclusion that it is in their self-interest to make such large changes to their culture and lifestyle. At some future time, the KWS may see some virtue in spinning off the partnership division into a separate agency equal to the KWS in size and structure and which embraces a community development mandate. This new structure could then work with the KWS and its bio-diversity goal as an equal partner and not simply as a means of achieving the bio-diversity mandate.

What is needed now is a strategic plan outlining the details of implementation of the fine set of policies outlined in the KWS conceptual plan of June 1997 (KWS,1997). Implementation plans are still being developed by the group ranches, so the quality of these strategies is yet unknown. While creating the appropriate atmosphere in which these plans will develop, the KWS has not engaged in an extensive training program to assist the group ranches with this complex activity. This may prove to be the weakness of the project requiring future attention.

Expanding the work of the KWS

The purpose of this research is to examine a very successful attempt at bringing local communities and other stakeholders into partnership with the national body responsible for the national parks and the tourism function. While analysis and critique of the KWS operation is important to that goal, it is not the only activity of this research. The major question to be addressed is: what lessons can be learned from this progressive organization which can be applied in a general way to other African initiatives attempting to preserve wildlife and enhance the welfare of their people? We truly believe the KWS can serve as an example and help advance other planning processes for bio-diversity development and greater environmental preservation.

Following from this discussion, a model can begin to be constructed for community based tourism development in Africa. Any such model would need to include the items identified in Figure 4.2.

Figure 4.2 Community Based Tourism Development Model

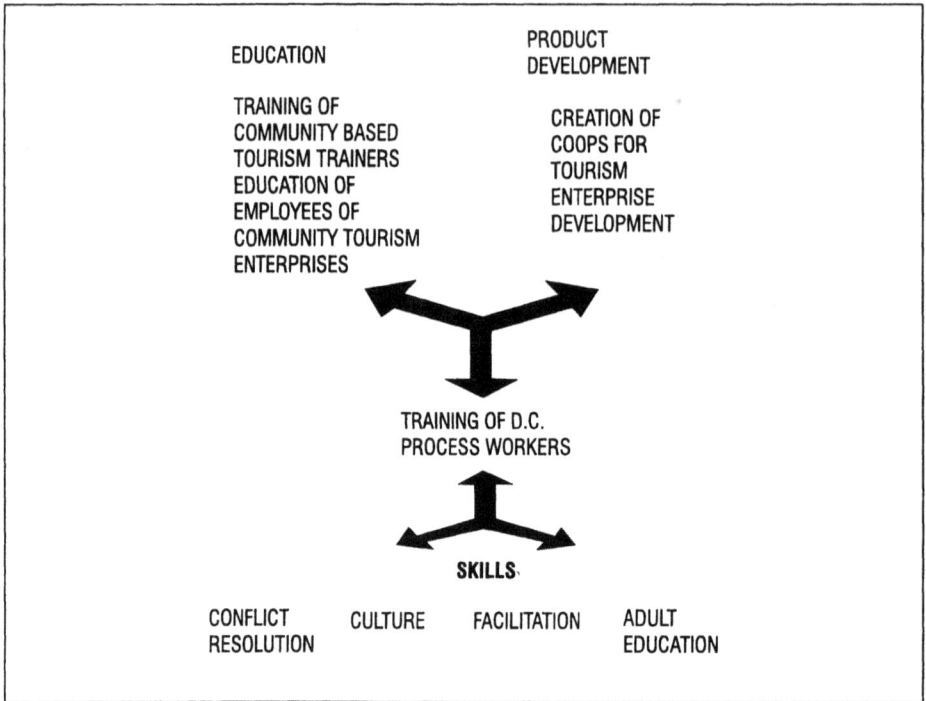

EDUCATION | PRODUCT DEVELOPMENT

TRAINING OF COMMUNITY BASED TOURISM TRAINERS EDUCATION OF EMPLOYEES OF COMMUNITY TOURISM ENTERPRISES

CREATION OF COOPS FOR TOURISM ENTERPRISE DEVELOPMENT

TRAINING OF D.C. PROCESS WORKERS

SKILLS

CONFLICT RESOLUTION | CULTURE | FACILITATION | ADULT EDUCATION

The model outlined here is a framework which can be applied in many African countries as they attempt to develop ecotourism as a tool for environmental preservation and economic development in rural areas. The model is based on the principle of equal partnership between a national or extra-national organization and the local community. The model focuses on gearing up the community to be an equal participating partner. The problems and concerns found in this research are so basic that they are likely to be relevant to most African countries. In order to give the model some practical flavour, however, it will be developed and addressed in the Kenyan context.

The model put forward here centers on four fundamental areas: general education of the population; specific education of direct line workers involved in the tourism enterprise; continued development of the product for both size and quality; and process skill development for those who are charged with integrating the product and service at the community and regional level.

Training and education

The research determined that continued focus on a broad education of rural people is still an important consideration in any development work, and particularly for tourism development. While this should be an ongoing goal, specific focus should be placed on people who are already involved in the tourism industry. Subjects for consideration should include basic literacy and numeracy skills and extend to such areas as business skills, accounting, cross-cultural training, and tourism practices. Most of this training should take place at the community level. While formal training is provided in the national hospitality and hotel schools, on-the-job training will always be important because most of the direct contact with tourists will be made by community people such as curio hawkers who do not have formal training.

The key to the success of this proposal lies in attracting the right people to train others. Many community people encountered during this research could fill that role. Some were retired teachers, others were high-level employees in hotels and lodges, and others worked for NGOs. People who are educated and highly respected and trusted in the community should be sought out for this role. The August 12, 1997 KWS/stakeholder workshop, referred to earlier in this chapter, discussed the private sector's potential role in tourism development and this training could certainly be a primary contribution for them. Once potential trainers have been identified, they should be given intensive trainers' training before filling this role. A one- or two-week workshop in a facility such as the KWS Naivasha Wildlife Training Institute would be an ideal site. The KWS should consider negotiating with the appropriate stakeholders to share funds for this purpose.

Product development

Ongoing product development is a concern. There did not appear to be any comprehensive strategy for on-the-ground community tourism development. Most documents and attention focused on the national parks. It is reported that a draft tourism development strategy has been developed by the Japanese International Co-operation Agency (JICA), but because it is not yet in the public domain, it was not available for this research.

It makes some sense to plan tourism development from a regional perspective. For example, visitors should be encouraged to visit the many non-park sanctuaries in the Amboseli region. Kimana and the Kilimanjaro mountain are two prime examples, along with many *manyattas*, which can offer a cultural opportunity. A local network of lodges, tour and safari operators should be established to create a regional destination identity. While many of these businesses see themselves as competitors, they are also allies in development. They have more to gain by joining forces cooperatively than by remaining isolated. They should also take a hand in developing and shaping the community enterprises to augment their own programming. Many of their visitors would appreciate a community visit which includes a cultural tourism experience. This side of the tourism business is the least developed. While lodges may offer local dance performances, visitors would also like to explore some of the fascinating Maasai culture.

Continued product development must be as much a concern as the already highly developed marketing efforts if Kenya and other African countries are going to remain competitive in the worldwide tourism marketplace. While the wildlife on which Kenya and other parts of Africa have based their tourism is impressive, the tourist is now looking for an authentic, unique, and wide-ranging educational experience. Those responsible for tourism will need to be imaginative in product development which encompasses more than their countries' natural endowments. Special requirements also need to be considered. A case in point is the Elder Hostel travel programme, which is geared to serving senior citizens, the fastest growing demographic group in developed countries. Product development also includes the infrastructure on which tourism relies. In Kenya's case, attention should be given to road network and infrastructure improvement.

Leadership in this area could come from the KWS regional tourism personnel in each of the KWS regional offices. However, they would require additional training and a well thought-out strategic plan specifying detailed actions and desired outcomes.

Community development process workers

Integrating the activities of training and product development is an important task and cannot be left to chance. With basic, ongoing community development, such concerns as capacity building, continuous identification and clarification of community issues, and establishment of community processes to solve community problems are paramount. Process consultation requires personnel with a specific set of skills, so it is not productive to engage people who are not properly trained for the job. This position is charged with overseeing and bringing the training and product development aspects of the model together in an integrated process at the community or regional level. The KWS regional partnership people are in a position to provide this process consultation service but would need special, additional training to be effective. Most of the people in these positions are formally trained in the wildlife area and would need further training in a different skill set to initiate what is being suggested here.

Who is best positioned to do this work?

As stated above, there does not appear to be an organization of the same size or the historical perspective as the KWS which has a mandate to undertake community development work. It must be stressed that unless equal attention is given to the community development from a social, health and educational point of view, the partnership project may not achieve its desired outcome.

It is not realistic to suggest that a single organization could be created to undertake such a task, so the next best solution might be to develop a coalition of both Kenyan and foreign community development NGOs. The KWS would need to provide leadership to this thrust as well as some seed money. The coalition of agencies could then act in concert with the KWS to realize maximum benefit for both interests. Some consideration should be given to spinning off the KWS partnership division into an agency that could stand alone to perform this function. However, resources equal to the task would need to be provided. Perhaps equal sharing of revenue from the tourism section of the enterprise might be considered and/or other sources found.

CONCLUSION

The recent reorganization of the Kenya Wildlife Service, which created a partnership division headed by an Assistant Director, appears to be insightful and a strategy which could be instructive to many African countries. The KWS may not have gone far enough, however. Until community development becomes as important as bio-diversity and other goals, the desired outcome may be muted. Relationships of a symbiotic nature must be created and conflict over resource use reduced. Tourism has a potential role in this regard. Communities can increase their standard of living by engaging in tourism. Tourism in this part of the world rests mainly on bio-diversity and culture. As people begin to understand that principle, they will gain new reverence for the natural world around them. This is what is meant by symbiosis, two organisms living in conjunction with each other to their mutual advantage.

REFERENCES

Ashley, C. 1995: *Tourism Communities and the Potential Impacts on Local Incomes and Conservation.* Windhoek: Directorate of Environmental Affairs, Ministry of Environment and Tourism.

Ashley, C. and Garland, E. 1994: *Promoting Community Based Tourism Development: Why, What and How?* Windhoek: Directorate of Environmental Affairs, Ministry of Environment and Tourism.

Berger, D. 1993: *Wildlife Extension: Participatory Conservation by the Maasai in Kenya.* Nairobi: African Centre for Technology Studies.

Kenya Wildlife Service. 1996: *Wildlife Policy, 1996.* Nairobi: Government Printer.

Kenya Wildlife Service. 1997: *Maintaining Bio-diversity into the 21st Century: A Conceptual Paper.* Nairobi: Government Printer.

Keesing, R.M. and Keesing, F.M. 1971: *New Perspectives in Cultural Anthropology.* New York: Holt, Rinehart and Winston.

Republic of Kenya. 1997: *Eighth National Development Plan.* Nairobi: Government Printer.

Talbot, L. and Olindo, P. 1990: The Maasai Mara and Amboseli Reserves. In A. Kiss (ed.), *Living With Wildlife: Wildlife Resource Management with Local Participation in Africa,* pp. 67-74. Washington, D.C.: The World Bank.

Western, D. 1982: Amboseli National Park: Enlisting Land Owners to Conserve Migratory Wildlife. *Ambio,* 11 (5), 302-308.

Chapter 5

SUSTAINING HUMAN AND AVIAN POPULATIONS IN MOZAMBIQUE: THE NEED FOR ECOTOURISM

by Dan Nuttall

INTRODUCTION

In the post-war setting of Mozambique, we are confronted by the "casualty of landscape" (Nuttall, 1998a). It is eerily silent in the national parks, where armies once set up bases. More than 90% of the wildlife that could provide sustenance or profit has been killed. A returning tide of 3 million displaced people advances across the landscape affecting everything in its path. Smaller vertebrate wildlife, unnoticed during the war, is now disappearing as the traditional use of wildlife resources has resumed. Small, scattered wildlife populations still exist in this country where much of the flora and smaller fauna have never been thoroughly inventoried.

Whether forest, farm, bare, burning, or dotted with traditional homes, the landscape bears witness to all that has passed and continues to speak as a testimonial to survival. Here, just under mother earth's skin, are hundreds of thousands of land mines. The slow task of land mine removal continues.

People are now finding the freedom to move, to farm, and to engage in a diverse economy. With over 2700 km of pristine and sandy coastline, mangrove swamps, significant marine food resources, and more rainfall than many other African countries, Mozambique stands poised at the brink of everything the future has to offer – and the future, most assuredly, means development.

Both the potential and the responsibility for development are enormous. In its various guises, development moves quickly – and mistakes, if any, will occur at the same pace.

One thing is obvious: Mozambique's vast resources present a rare potential for much needed socio-economic benefit, as well as an opportunity to learn from the mistakes of Sub-Saharan neighbours. The blank canvas of development awaits the artistry of the Mozambican people. But what form should this artistry of development assume?

Given the current socio-economic status of Mozambique (among the world's ten poorest countries) and the potential for further destruction of wildlife resources, both progressive environmental policy and low-impact, community-based initiatives should be viewed as a means of providing economic gain while conserving bio-diversity. Examples of successful low-impact tourism ventures in other African countries should be seriously considered.

This chapter presents, as an example, the sustainable integration of a small localized population of a threatened bird species, the olive-headed weaver (*Ploceus Olivaceiceps*), and a local human population within the context of low-impact tourism. The goal of this integration is to provide local opportunities for livelihood diversification, while conserving bio-diversity. The anticipated scenario is one of bird-watching as a form of ecotourism. A description of methodology and research setting is provided, followed by a discussion of the ecotourism context as a vehicle for development. Subsequently, the chapter describes the roles of three major stakeholders – the bird, the people and the landscape. Finally, the chapter discusses some ways in which all of the stakeholders can benefit by using a multi-dimensional "lens" to examine relationships between stakeholders in the context of ecotourism.

RESEARCH SETTING AND METHODOLOGY

This research arose out of a need identified by the Republic of Mozambique's Ministerio da Agricultura e Pescas (Ministry of Agriculture and Fisheries) in conjunction with the Endangered Wildlife Trust, the only conservation non-governmental organization (NGO) in Mozambique. The mission of the Trust is to "conserve the diversity of species in southern Africa" (Journal of the EWT, 1997). As a part of this commitment to conserving diversity, the Trust has undertaken the preparation of the "Mozambican Bird Atlas", a geographic analysis of the distribution of bird species in Mozambique. During the preparation of this atlas, it was discovered that the one confirmed population of a little known bird species, the olive-headed weaver (*Ploceus Olivaceiceps*), was perceived to be dwindling. The larger distribution of the bird was unknown. The reasons for their dwindling population were also unknown, as nothing was known about the bird. With financial assistance from the Environmental Capacity Enhancement Project (ECEP) and in collaboration with the Mozambican Government and other agencies, the author undertook research to determine the life-history traits of the weaver, the needs of local human communities, and the sustainable integration of both in the context of ecotourism.

The research took place approximately 23 km southwest of Panda, a small town in Inhambane Province in southern Mozambique. The research area lies just outside the boundary of the Tropic of Capricorn (23.5 degrees south of the equator), in tropical, humid, deciduous miombo forests. Two vegetative forms dominate, with large deciduous *Brachystegia* trees providing a loose but almost continuous canopy, and, beneath them, a monoculture of grass interspersed with loose sand.

Given the threatened status of the weaver and its small population size, field research methods were chosen to be as humane and non-invasive as possible. Field research methodology was consistent with "category B" experiments which cause "little or no discomfort or stress" as outlined by the Canadian Council on Animal Care (CCAC, 1991). Research activities such as behavioural observations, collection of faecal samples, and retrieval of abandoned nests were all completed with little or no disturbance to the bird population. Given the sensitive research context, the lack of information on the species and paucity of nesting sites, a more qualitative and "classical" approach to understanding the life-history requirements of the olive-headed weaver was undertaken. In addition to an overall historical summary of research related to the species, the following life-history traits of the weaver were considered: distribution, density and population size, morphology (size, weight, appearance), geographic location of nests, nest attributes, nest tree attributes, vegetative characteristics of nest tree area, nesting activity, foraging behaviour patterns and diet.

An understanding of the potential distribution of the weaver was gained through a largely historical analysis of preserved avian collections, academic and non-academic publications and personal communications. While a more comprehensive, *in situ* methodology is required, the current study had neither the funds nor the logistical support to undertake such a study. Given that the primary goal was to develop an understanding of the bird's life-history traits, the researcher chose to focus on a location which offered the greatest possible chance of locating the bird, which was revealed to be in a forest near the town of Panda.

Again, given the unique setting and pioneering nature of this work, an understanding of local human community needs was gained through exploratory interviews using directed conversation. Interviews were generally held at the homesteads of local families, with all family members present. Most often it was the oldest male in the household who answered questions in the presence of other family members who contributed periodically. Some interviews were held separately with women, although in general this was difficult to negotiate.

THE CONTEXT OF ECOTOURISM

The form of low-impact tourism suggested here is more commonly known as "ecotourism". Ecotourism is defined by the Ecotourism Society as responsible travel that conserves the natural environment and sustains the well being of local people (USAID, 1992). Boo (1990) broadens this definition, suggesting that ecotourism is nature travel that actually contributes to conservation. It contributes to conservation by generating funds for protected areas, creating employment opportunities for communities surrounding protected areas, and providing environmental education for visitors.

Moving beyond definitions, it is particularly critical to situate ecotourism within the global economy and identify its potential for positive economic impact in developing countries. Tourism is one of world's leading industries at US$2 trillion dollars (Edgell, 1990) and is the world's largest employer. Within this leading industry, ecotourism is the fastest growing sector. According to the United States Agency for International Development (1992, p.1), "there is no doubt as to the desirability of developing tourism as a vehicle that can lead to sustainable and equitable economic development, conservation, bio-diversity, and social benefits in African countries".

Economic returns in Rwanda may be used as an example. Lindbergh (1991) describes one million dollars in entrance fees and two to three million dollars in other expenditures in Rwanda. The majority of these funds are related to ecotourism surrounding mountain gorillas in the Virungas. The income generating potential of low-impact tourism has also been evaluated using other methodologies. In Amboseli National Park in Kenya, for example, a researcher estimated the gross monetary values for several wildlife species. Each lion was estimated to be worth US$27,000 per annum, while the elephant herd was estimated at US$610,000 per annum in tourist revenues. The values were based solely on the value of non-consumptive viewing activities (Boo, 1990). These revenue values exceed the value of goods obtained through traditional agricultural practises.

Notwithstanding these figures, a more holistic interpretation of the benefits of low-impact tourism may provide more arguable outcomes. In many areas of the world, the establishment of protected areas has involved the displacement of indigenous communities and little or no participation in development of ecotourism. Note that in Boo's definition of ecotourism, she speaks of creating employment opportunities for communities *surrounding* protected areas as if communities *never* reside within the boundaries of conservation areas (Ghimire, 1991). In addition, the funds generated by low-impact tourism often do not reach local communities but either "leak" out of the country to support "foreigners" or are absorbed by various levels of government. In Nepal, the rapid growth of "ecotourism", combined with a rapid population growth, created a crisis of "[p]oaching of wildlife and timber, littering and other problems exacerbated by the numerous visitors...there was a heavy toll on the environment and its local human inhabitants" (Hummel, 1994, p. 17). The goal must be to ensure that socio-economic benefits are local or regional and that the links between human, animal and landscape cultures are not severed but are sustained.

The success of an ecotourism approach to conserving bio-diversity will depend on a variety of factors, among which are the faunal characteristics of the site. Using a modified version of Nuttall's "AAC" (Nuttall, 1993) or "Animal-As-Client" approach, we can suggest that the success of a single species approach to conservation and ecotourism will depend on the development or designation of an environment which considers the animal as the starting point and focus of the design process:

> "Designers and managers of [conservation areas] require: an understanding of the animal's life-history stages, life-history events, behavioural pattern types and frequencies, movements in space and time, ways to increase [genetic] fitness and methods of determining and meeting animal needs" (ibid., p. 215).

This research is such a starting point. If our goals to conserve bio-diversity and provide local economic benefit are to be realized, we must begin by developing an understanding of the life-history traits of the focal species, the olive-headed weaver. Our knowledge of all stakeholders – the bird, the people and the landscape – will allow us to achieve balance in ecotourism development. At the same time, the knowledge will serve to maintain a "connection" between the human population and the bird/landscape complex, something which is viewed as integral to sustainable development (Bryden, 1994). While many attributes of the bird and human populations and the landscape could be described, this chapter will limit discussion to only a few.

The bird

This study's bird population inhabits the forest adjacent to the small town of Panda. A small perching songbird about the size of a house sparrow, it is currently known only in the tropical deciduous forests of southern Mozambique (Clancey, 1996; Parker, personal communication, September, 1993). Historically, the species has been widespread, ranging from northeastern Tanzania through southern Malawi into northern, central and southern Mozambique. Throughout this distribution area, the population has never been continuous but has existed and located in small isolated populations. Records of sightings and collection of specimens have been minimal. Within the study area, the bird appears to be unique in several respects.

The olive-headed weaver requires mature *Brachystegia* forests (Nuttall, 1998b). This tree is a tropical deciduous species which reaches a maximum height of about 18 metres and a diameter at breast height (dbh) of about 40 cm. In these trees, the bird builds its nests entirely out of *Usnea Mexicana,* a species of lichen that we usually refer to as a "moss". The long, stringy and bedraggled appearance of this lichen has earned it the nickname "old man's beard". For many people, *Usnea* conjures up images of swamps and bayous with long skeins of lichen hanging from tree branches. In addition to displaying a rather narrow preference for habitat, the bird appears to be primarily an insectivore and is usually found foraging in the branches of mature *Brachystegia.* Typically, the bird moves along and around the branch in short hopping movements as it probes and gleans insect prey from the bark and beneath crustose and foliose lichens. Breeding season is from August to December. During this time, birds are easier to locate, as the trees are not in leaf and both birds and nests are more visible. While a preliminary suggestion would be that the bird is imperiled by habitat loss caused by humans, it is also possible that the bird may benefit, in part, from nearby human inhabitants who decrease the number of potential predators.

The people

In the olive-headed weaver's patch of forest, there live people who earn their livelihood from subsistence agriculture. Exploratory research involving conversations with local families and individuals revealed a variety of attributes of this community.

Most of the people engage in subsistence agriculture, cultivating corn, cassava, peanuts and beans. Some households have chickens, ducks, pigs, cattle and donkeys. Most of their food resources are entirely dependent upon the land owned by each household. While a diversity of crops and animals are cultivated, there are periods when, mostly due to drought, food supplies are low. The most difficult time of the year is August to December, when crops are not yet mature and some families do not have enough to eat. During these months, financial resources or trading are used to procure food. In addition to domestic animals, wild game is eaten whenever it is available and affordable. Family members may engage in hunting or purchase it from local hunters. A variety of animal resources are used, ranging from large antelope to fish and small forest birds. Plant resources are also collected from the forest and used for foodstuffs, personal hygiene and medicine. While some people use a variety of traditional herbal medicines or the services of a healer, many would prefer to use a hospital.

The *Brachystegia* tree has a variety of uses including the inner bark for rope, the red layer just below the bark for an emetic, and the wood for firewood and building materials.

Similarly, the lichen *Usnea* has several uses, mostly associated with its absorptive qualities, making it a useful material for personal hygiene.

Insufficient water supply, health care, transportation, schooling and jobs are primary issues facing the community. The political system and the understanding of it are variable. Interpretation of matters related to land use and harvesting of wildlife is variable. For example, some individuals spoke of hunting "seasons" while others hunted year round, some people said they would kill local hippos if they had a gun, while others said the hippos were protected by national laws. Some people said the government must be consulted in the process of obtaining land, while others said they simply took the land they wanted (ensuring they did not offend neighbours in doing so).

Knowledge of local wildlife and perceptions related to conservation are variable. The interviews revealed an overwhelming perception that the forest is limitless and that there will always be enough. In contrast, a few adults and the majority of young people feel it is important to save some of the forest for animals, for gathering medicines and to walk in.

There is no production of local goods other than hunted game and reed bundles for thatching roofs. To obtain funds, some (male) family members travel to South Africa, where they work in mines or drive taxis. They return home periodically and supplement the family income. Extra food produced is used as a form of commerce, usually in trade for other necessities such as sugar, salt, soap and medicines. While many of these products may be purchased at a local market, some items must be purchased from Panda, 25 km away. To reach Panda, people will walk, try to pick up a ride on the road where there is very little traffic, or pay for the local "taxi", a tractor which passes by twice a day.

The landscape

Mozambique receives a modest amount of rainfall every year, making crop production and procuring drinking water fairly dependable. Even so, there is often no surface water for many kilometres and well water may be several kilometres away from individual families, as was the case in this study. Crops maturation is most dependent upon the months of August to December when a limited "wet" season brings needed rains. If these rains do not arrive or do not provide adequate moisture, crops fail.

The forest is dominated by large *Brachystegia,* the size being attributed to the adequate rainfall and deep sands. The species is assumed to be *Brachystegia Spiciformis,* though it is important to note that taxonomically, the genus is probably the most difficult in Africa, given complicated patterns in variation and the tendency to hybridize (White, 1962). There are other tree and shrub species, though their numbers are limited. The *Brachystegia* forests, once disturbed, are thought to be prone to invasion and replacement by *Julbernardia Globiflora.*

The forest is interspersed with cultivated areas. The cultivated areas are cleared by "ring-barking" trees, cutting through the bark all the way around the tree trunk to disrupt the nutrient transport between the leafy canopy and the roots. After waiting six months to a year for the trees to die, the people burn the trees at the base until they fall down or can be pushed over. The trees are chopped up and used for firewood or sometimes for building. If trees are particularly large, they are left in the field and cultivation is initiated around them. There are areas of the forest which were previously cleared by a sawmill and are now regenerating.

The substrate is a loose Kalahari sand with a thin covering of grasses, forbs and vines. The surface is very sensitive to mechanical stress. Footpaths are easily maintained and it only requires two or three passes of a vehicle through the forest to leave a permanent trail.

The triad of birds, people and landscape in the context of ecotourism

The relationship between birds, people and landscape in the context of ecotourism is shown in Figure 5.1.

Figure 5.1 The triad of local bird population,
local human population, landscape, and their interactions
must be considered in the context (dashed line) of ecotourism

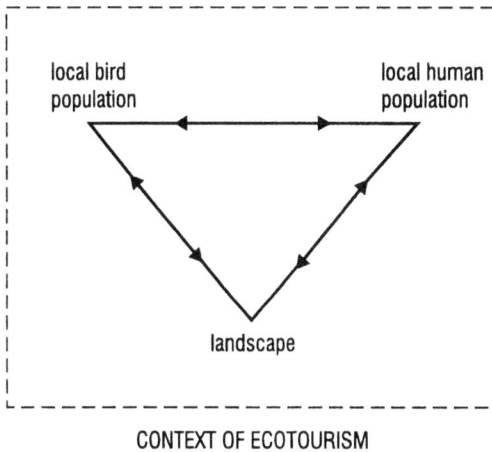

CONTEXT OF ECOTOURISM

There are three basic questions which should be asked of this relationship. The answers to these questions will allow us to modify the model and to suggest practical mechanisms for affecting the goal of sustaining all three players. The questions are:

▶ What is the fundamental paradigm shift that we seek to introduce to this existing relationship?
▶ How do we relate the components of the triad to each other?
▶ In the context of ecotourism, how does a paradigm shift change the way in which the components of the model relate?

The fundamental paradigm shift that we seek focuses on human communities, their perceptions and behaviour. The necessary change in perception is a shift from people thinking about the *uses* of landscape to thinking about the *need* for landscape (Figure 5.2).

Figure 5.2 Within the context of ecotourism, the relationship between the three components must be examined through a multi-dimensional lens which considers both positive and negative political (P) economic (E) social (S) cultural (C), and environmental (En) impacts

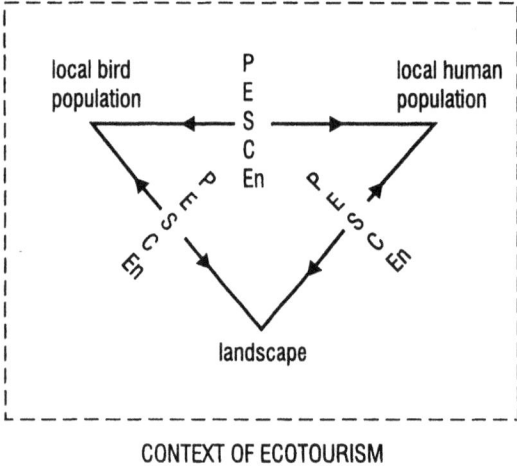

CONTEXT OF ECOTOURISM

The link between sustainable development and the necessary transformation of the human psyche has been described by other authors (Kellman & Tackaberry, 1997). The idea of dependence and resource provision versus consumption is the fundamental paradigm shift required. Critical to this idea is the concept of sustaining a dependable resource base to provide future resources. Such resources may be offered to the paying public at rates which exceed the long-term combined values of other forest-based commercial transactions.

The components of the triad may be related to each other through a multi-dimensional "lens" (Figure 5.2). The dimensions contributing to each lens include political, economic, social, cultural and environmental (PESCEn) dimensions.

The triad of people, landscape and birds is interactive and co-dependent. Using the setting of ecotourism and the specific examples of the weaver and local human population attributes, an examination of pair-wise relationships allows for the identification of interactions which could provide either positive or negative (or both) outcomes. These analyses occur through the multi-dimensional lens (PESCEn: P = political, E = economic, S = Social, C = cultural, En = environmental dimensions, - and + indicate potential negative and positive impacts respectively). Selected examples of pair-wise relationships and their potential for positive or negative impacts include:

People and Birds: As people consume the bird or remove habitat, bio-diversity is reduced (-En). As bio-diversity decreases, the "rift" between people and landscape widens, creating a condition that contributes to "unsustainability" (Bryden, 1994). Conversely, people might participate in ecotourism. By conserving the bird species and larger bio-diversity they may realize economic benefits which, in turn, contribute to local community improvements, such as, employment, education, medical services and transportation (+En, +E, +S, +C). An alternative might be to approach conservation through legislation. While governmental agencies could protect the bird through legislation, this would be viewed as a negative form of interaction between people and the bird. It is not a "ground-up" approach, involves no education or change in perception/behaviour, and is difficult to enforce (-P).

People and Landscape: People can reduce their dependence upon land (+En) in the immediate vicinity by engaging in ecotourism. This allows the community to engage in financial transactions for the same resources produced elsewhere, widening the economic net in a ripple effect. In addition, as more and more land is deforested and used for agriculture, it takes more travel time and costs more to obtain wild game, herbal medicines and other forest products (-E). Ultimately, protecting the forest and bird populations may allow for sustainable use of some resources for food and medicine while conserving bio-diversity (+En, +E, +C, +S). Alternate industries which create air-borne pollutants may destroy lichen populations over a widespread area and prohibit nesting, ultimately destroying bird populations (-En). Again, given Mozambique's larger socio-economic context and the need for education, employment and conservation, connecting human community networks to landscape through developing a lichen population bio-monitoring programme might be a cost-effective means of monitoring pollution.

Lichen may be used as an indicator of ecosystem "health", providing a low-cost means of assessing gross atmospheric conditions (+En). Additional considerations in this section of the triad would address the sensitivity of the local substrate to mechanical pressure (-En), suggesting that increased numbers of people walking through the forest may have a negative impact. A strategy developed in response to this would be directed at ecotourists, as local communities constantly reuse existing paths. Finally, the ecotourism development scenario could investigate additional strategies for marketing locally manufactured or collected goods (+En, +E, +C).

Landscape and Bird: The bird is completely dependent upon the lichen *Usnea* for nesting material. Such specialization is judged to be negative as the bird is less adaptable (-En). Furthermore, the lichen may be completely dependent upon mature *Brachystegia* trees as a substrate for colonization, again showing a narrow niche in terms of host suitability (-En). The bird is largely dependent upon insects for its diet. Any alteration to the landscape such as the addition of pesticides and herbicides would threaten the bird species (-En). These factors suggest that sustaining landscape could contribute to conserving trees, lichen, insect and bird populations (+E). Any forms of industry that create atmospheric pollutants which can be carried for many kilometres would be discouraged (-E). An analysis of wind direction, speed and possible distribution of effluents should be mandatory as an environmental assessment in this district.

SYNTHESIS: ECOTOURISM AND ITS STAKEHOLDERS

The goal of a synthesis is to minimize the number of negative impacts, while maximizing the number of positive impacts in the triad. There are many possible outcomes which should be discussed within the context of the multi-dimensional lens in Figure 5.2. From a political perspective, the Mozambican government should be involved in development which considers local contexts and local solutions. There must be "bottom-up" and participatory approaches to ensure that community needs are assessed and community support drives the process. Given that communities are sceptical of such intervention, they must participate in both creating and realizing concrete, obtainable goals which directly benefit local communities.

The potential for economic impact at local and international levels merits serious consideration. In Costa Rica, for example, tourism contributed 29% of total exports in 1993, a contribution that exceeded banana production at 27% (Aylward, Allen, Echeverria and Tosi, 1996).

Given Mozambique's poverty, the economic dimension is most critical. Ecotourism offers an opportunity to contribute forest resources (plants, building material, and medicines) to a sustainable effort, while an opportunity for viewing bird species, particularly the olive-headed weaver, generates cash flow. In the long term, forest conservation may contribute to the economic needs of future generations through the development of plant-based medicines.

The triad also suggests a unique trade-off during times of food shortage, August through December. During this period the bird is breeding and the trees are not in leaf, creating an ideal setting for locating weavers and other bird species. Ecotourism income during this period could offset starvation in the community. Communities could also investigate the possibility of producing hand-crafted goods to sell to ecotourists.

From a socio-cultural perspective, ecotourism development must recognize that traditional religions and ceremonies are intimately linked to landscape. The preservation of landscape is the preservation of culture. Conserving land contributes to conservation of both knowledge and resources to be used in the future during drought or famine. Proceeds from ecotourism could be used to expand local educational opportunities which, in turn, could emphasize the link between humans, landscape and sustainability. In the short term, this must include participatory workshops for adults involved in land related decision-making – but who perceive the landscape as "limitless". Such workshops could play a critical role in presenting ecotourism as a development option. The workshops could emphasize the sustainable relationships between culture and landscape (medicine, foodstuffs, hunting, daily travel for resource collection), and economics and landscape. The potential benefits of ecotourism should be introduced to the community with an emphasis on community-based and community-determined priorities (water, health care, food security, education). Costs, benefits, timing and long-term goals must be emphasized so that there are rational expectations.

Both birds and people are linked through the landscape which sustains them. This landscape is sensitive to erosion and disturbance, so ecotourist movement within the landscape must be minimized.

Further, ecotourism development must include local community awareness as to how they can protect their forest from deterioration by outside forces. If industry is established leading to deforestation, forest alteration, or air pollution, community efforts towards sustainable ecotourism will be futile. Communities must enter into dialogue with local, provincial and national governments and demonstrate the long-term benefits of ecotourism versus industry. To this end, the community must draw up a physical and logistical plan for the protected area, including:

▶ established boundaries;
▶ suitable places and times for observing the olive-headed weaver;
▶ protected nesting areas;
▶ establishing quantities, types and areas where forest resources can be harvested sustainably;
▶ a schedule which considers the timing of birding in relation to food scarcity (emphasizing months of August to December when food security is low and bird is breeding);
▶ minimizing movement within the protected area due to sensitive substrate;
▶ management of funds received.

It is recommended that a community committee be formed requiring more than one signature, and that consensus be required for approval of funds disbursement. The community must determine if any additional funding will be needed to increase food production through the use of fertilizers or pesticides. Sustainable, alternative and non-toxic strategies should be exhausted first. The impact of toxins on the food chain should be considered, particularly the insect fauna upon which the bird is dependent.

Two final points must be made about the conservation of larger bio-diversity and how this relates to conservation of the olive-headed weaver. First, threatened bird species tend to be coincidental with centres of avian species richness among African tropical forest species (Crowe & Crowe, 1982). This means that conservation of the olive-headed weaver may be coincidental with conserving an area rich with other bird species. Second, where there are threatened bird species, there are threatened ecosystems (Beissinger, Steadman, Wohlgenant, Blate and Zack, 1996). By protecting threatened bird species we are also protecting threatened ecosystems and their threatened flora and fauna.

CONCLUSION

In the forests near Panda, Mozambique, the potential positive impacts of ecotourism in the form of bird-watching should not be underestimated. The focus on a threatened species, the olive-headed weaver, and its life-history traits has revealed a unique and highly dependent relationship with several components of landscape (mature *Brachystegia* trees, *Usnea* as sole nest building material for nests, insects for diet). In the unique, post-war setting of Mozambique, the landscape is inextricably linked to a human culture with limited options for livelihood and a dependence upon forest resources for food, medicine and building materials. The question of competition arises: how can stakeholders maintain and benefit from their relationships? Based on the current understanding of the life-history traits of the olive-headed weaver and local human populations, the following recommendations for conservation in an ecotourism context are offered:

- Set aside a protected area (sustainable forest resource area, SFRA) and consider protection of supporting ecosystems for the species (possible scenario of protection on a watershed/aquifer basis). Consider the implementation of "sanctuary areas" where human interference is minimized within the larger SFRA;
- Develop quantifiable economic models that link landscape, bird and human populations. The model must factor in the consumptive and non-consumptive "values" of forest resource products which are used by local human communities;
- Ensure a multi-dimensional, integrated development approach based upon a "bottom-up" and local community approach in the formation of such a protected area. Develop an ecotourism steering committee with members from local communities, chiefs, government officials, as well as tour operators;
- Develop an understanding of and improve relations between government, NGOs and the travel industry within the larger context of national ecotourism initiatives. A profile of Sub-Saharan ecotourism successes and failures should be given priority and used to develop a series of guidelines within which national ecotourism is developed;
- Ensure that future development does not include industry which produces nitrogen or sulphur-based aerial emissions. Undertake studies of wind direction and potential fallout areas for industries producing aerial pollutants;

- Manage the protected area in a manner that provides a continuous supply of mature *Brachystegia* trees, which in turn provides a suitable substrate for colonization by *Usnea;*
- Consider community-based bio-monitoring of *Usnea* populations as a baseline project for monitoring atmospheric pollutants throughout the range of suitable lichens;
- Manage forests to ensure that *Brachystegia* dominant stands are maintained. Competition or invasion by other tree species, such as *Julbernardia* and cashew trees introduced through agriculture, should be minimized. These trees may not be able to provide a suitable substrate for colonization by *Usnea;*
- Develop education programs for local communities, local workers and ecotourists. Local community education should be effected at the curriculum level to achieve the widest support from current and future community members. Obtain funding for and direct ecotourism funds toward education of local individuals to create wildlife officials or conservation officers;
- Ensure that watershed or aquifer-based management consider the possible effects of introduced pesticides, herbicides or fertilizers on local flora and fauna, particularly food chains affecting insectivorous species such as the olive-headed weaver;
- Fund multi-dimensional research to further understand the political, economic, social, cultural and environmental links between stakeholders. Research into carrying capacity, conservation of local human culture and customs, social impacts of tourism, and feasibility of local artisan products should be undertaken.

Because ecotourism is an integrated option, it presents a highly positive alternative for livelihood diversification, economic and social benefit and bio-diversity conservation. Ecotourism relies upon landscape, its biotic and abiotic components, its energy and nutrient cycles, as well as its visible and not-so-visible components. Ecotourism can sustain and protect dependent relationships and manipulate them to provide multi-dimensional support for local human populations, providing a win-win situation.

Our knowledge of both the bird and local human population allows us to search for context-dependent sustainable links. We see the coincidence of the period when the local human population's food supply is scarce and the olive-headed weaver is nesting and most visible. The local community has an opportunity to conserve bio-diversity, while generating ecotourism income when it is most needed to purchase food. While this discrete example demonstrates a capacity for environmentally and socially sound long-term economic growth, further understanding of birds, people and landscape is required.

In summary, our exploration of the bird, of landscape, and our knowledge of people and place, provides the answers which, of course, were always there. As Frost (1981) once said, nature is always hinting at us. It hints over and over again. And suddenly, we take the hint.

REFERENCES

Aylward, B., Allen, K., Echeverria, J. and Tosi, J. 1996: Sustainable Ecotourism in Costa Rica. *Bio-diversity and Conservation,* 5, 315-343.

Beissinger, S.R., Steadman, E.C., Wohlgenant, T., Blate, G. and Zack, S. 1996: Null Models for Assessing Ecosystem Conservation Priorities: Threatened Birds as Titres of Threatened Ecosystems in South America. *Conservation Biology,* 10 (5), 1343-1352.

Boo, E. 1990: *Ecotourism: The Potentials and Pitfalls.* Maryland: World Wildlife Fund.

Bryden, J. 1994: Towards Sustainable Rural Communities: From Theory to Action. In J.M. Bryden (ed.), *Towards Sustainable Rural Communities,* pp. 211-233. Guelph: University of Guelph Seminar series.

Canadian Council on Animal Care. 1991: Categories of Invasiveness in Animal Experiments. In University of Guelph (ed.), *Animal Utilization Protocol, Animal Care Committee,* pp. 8-9. Guelph: University of Guelph.

Clancey, P.A. 1996: *The Birds of Southern Mozambique.* Westville: African Bird Book Publishing.

Crowe, T.M. and Crowe, A.A. 1982: Patterns of distribution and endemism in Afrotropical birds. *J. Zool., Lond,* 198, 417-442.

Edgell, D. 1990: *Charting a Course for International Tourism in the Nineties: An Agenda for Managers and Executives.* Washington, D.C.: U.S. Department of Commerce, U.S. Travel and Tourism Administration and Economic Development Administration.

Frost, R. 1981. In: *The Audubon Notebook.* Rexdale: John Wiley & Sons Canada Ltd.

Ghimire, K.B. 1991: Parks & People: *Livelihood Issues in National Parks Management in Thailand and Madagascar.* Geneva: United Nations Research Institute for Social Development.

Hummel, J. 1994: Ecotourism Development in Protected Areas of Developing Countries. *World Leisure and Recreation,* 36 (2), 17-23.

Journal of The Endangered Wildlife Trust. 1997: Mission Statement. *Journal of the Endangered Wildlife Trust,* 25, 1.

Kellman, M. and Tackaberry, R. 1997: *Tropical Environments – The Functioning and Management of Tropical Ecosystems.* New York: Routledge.

Lindbergh, K. 1991: *Policies for Maximizing Nature Tourism's Ecological and Economic Benefits.* World Resources Institute, International Conservation Financing Project working paper.

Nuttall, D. 1998a: War and Peace and Wildlife in Mozambique – The Olive-headed Weaver Story. *Journal of the Endangered Wildlife Trust,* 28 (spring), 4-9.

Nuttall, D. 1998b: Olive-headed Weaver: In Search of the Living Nest. *Africa Birds & Birding,* 3 (1), 37-42.

Nuttall, D.B. 1993: *The Design of Optimal Environments for Displaced Animals: Theory and Application at the Metro Toronto Zoo, Master of Landscape Architecture Thesis.* Guelph: School of Landscape Architecture, University of Guelph.

United States Agency for International Development (Bureau for Africa). 1992: *Ecotourism: A Viable Alternative for Sustainable Management of Natural Resources in Africa.* USAID, International Resources Group, Office of Analysis, Research and Technical Support, Food Agriculture and Resource Analysis.

White, F. 1962: *Forest Flora of Northern Rhodesia.* Oxford: Oxford University Press.

Chapter 6

ENVIRONMENTAL PERCEPTIONS AND ATTITUDES OF FISHERY RESOURCE USERS AT STRUIS BAY, SOUTH AFRICA

by Lois Lindsay, Reid Kreutzwiser and Vincent Taylor

INTRODUCTION

This chapter will contextualize and describe the qualitative research on environmental perceptions and attitudes of fishery resource users in the town of Struis Bay, South Africa, which was undertaken in 1997 and 1998. This study was primarily concerned with the often divergent perceptions of the local fishery resource held by members of culturally and racially distinct groups in the town, where a burgeoning tourism industry, a dwindling natural resource, and the social and psychological legacies of apartheid combine to create a particularly challenging community development scenario. The chapter will briefly introduce the field of perception and attitude studies, and will provide an outline of the theoretical and empirical backgrounds to the research. After the political and site-specific contexts of the study are summarized, the research design and the methodologies by which data were obtained will be described and explained. Finally, this paper will present analysis and results of the research.

The trend towards economic, institutional, technological and communicational globalization has led to unprecedented degrees of inter-cultural contact, which in turn prompt either competition for, or attempted co-management of, natural resources by parties from vastly different cultures (e.g. Burdge, 1996; Edelstein and Kleese, 1995). Nature-based or ecotourism development is only one scenario in which the misunderstanding or deliberate ignorance of social and cultural differences among groups can precipitate mismanagement and conflict on various scales. Intimately tied to these practical considerations, however, are the philosophical and moral imperatives for justice which have particular salience in cross-cultural situations. In such cases, power differentials are a virtual inevitability, and the equitable distribution of ecological benefits and impacts among groups is of paramount concern.

There are perhaps few places where these issues are of more immediate and obvious importance than in South Africa. That country's history of racial segregation and uneven distribution of social, material and natural resources has created uniquely challenging policy-making and management situations for South Africa's new leadership.

THE RESEARCH PROBLEM

In the town of Struis Bay, two broadly-defined categories of fishery resource user groups can be identified.

The first are local-commercial fishers, permanent residents of the town, most of whom are "coloured," or of mixed race[1].

The other group are recreational fishers who are either "recreational-casual" fishers catching limited numbers of fish for their own consumption, or "recreational-commercial" fishers licenced to catch larger volumes of fish, and to put the catch on the local market. Both categories of recreational fishers are comprised largely of white professionals or retirees who fish during the holiday season (approximately November to February) and on weekends, and whose numbers are growing due to vacation home and tourism development in the region.

Over time, increased fishing pressure has reduced the number of commercially exploitable species in the area to a few seasonal shoal fish, the most important of which is yellowtail (*Seriola lalandi*) (Attwood and Bennett, 1995). During the summer, when the yellowtail run and the peak tourist season coincide, there is intense competition among user groups, and boats crowd on the shoals.

Many commercial fishers contend that the marketing activity of the recreational-commercial fishers – who are not economically dependent on the catch – has depressed market prices, severely hurting the incomes of local commercial fishers. In contrast to recreational fishers, the local commercial fishers depend heavily on the short yellowtail run for income and to repay debts accrued in the off-season (Taylor, personal communication, 1996, 1997).

Not surprisingly, conflict has arisen among these user groups. A better understanding of the ways in which members of each user group perceive the resource can contribute to the avoidance and resolution of such conflict in the future.

Research Goals and Objectives

Overarching research goal:

▶ to conduct a comparative study of the ways in which members of culturally distinct fishery user groups perceive and conceptualize the resource at Struis Bay, Western Cape Province, South Africa.

Research objectives:

▶ to *describe:*
  • the perceptions of the resource held by members of each user group (local-commercial, recreational-casual and recreational-commercial), with particular attention to the cultural significance of the resource and the perceptions thereof;
  • the current use of the fishery resource at Struis Bay by local commercial and recreational fishers;
  • the nature and extent of recent and current conflict among the user groups.
▶ to *analyze* the descriptive data by identifying:
  • trends and patterns of perceptions within and among user groups;
  • relationships among resource use, conflict over the resource, and perceptions of the resource.
▶ to *apply* the results in the generation of recommendations to ways in which a fuller understanding of the cultural differences among resource user groups might be incorporated into a culturally sensitive and sustainable tourism policy for Struis Bay, South Africa.

Research Context

Theoretical approaches to environmental perception and attitude studies

The theoretical underpinnings of this study spring from a tradition of humanistic approaches to the field, which examine the *experience* of landscape and lean away from positivism towards constructivism. Theoretical debate has centred around the concept of landscape and the role of culture in determining how we see, construct and assign meaning to our environments.

For the purpose of this research, a dynamic concept of the "cultural landscape" has been adopted, embodying not only the physical features of the landscape (both natural and human), but also an often unseen and ever-changing symbolic element imposed by human culture. The effort is thus to "historicize" and contextualize the landscape by studying the human and cultural elements which affect (and are affected by) it. Culture, rather than being either strictly produced by – or powerfully productive of – landscape, is seen by Jackson more as an arena or domain "in which social relations of dominance and subordination are negotiated and resisted, where meanings are not just imposed, but contested" (1989, p. 53; see also 1980). This perspective allows for human subjectivity and acknowledges the constant interplay among the natural, human and cultural elements.

While the above dynamic concept of the cultural landscape forms a part of the theoretical basis of this research, the notion of culture itself is also of crucial importance. For the purpose of this study, culture was conceptualized as a structured, traditional set of patterns for behaviour and thought which is specific to, though not uniform within, a given group (adapted from Zelinsky, 1992, p. 70). In lieu of a full theoretical discussion of the concept, several key elements of culture will instead be itemized.

First, in any large cultural group, there exist numerous overlapping sub-cultures to which a given individual may belong. Furthermore, culture is seen to be dynamic over time and space, and subject to alteration from both within and outside the group. Culture, including its production, its products, and its expression, is seen to be both affected by and constitutive of material, political and economic conditions or processes. Finally, while culture functions at a level which transcends the individual, it *also* operates at the individual level, providing people with, in Peter Jackson's (1993, p. 48) words, a medium through which to "transform the mundane phenomena of the material world into a world of significant symbols to which they give meaning and attach value". It is through this process that culture affects the environmental attitudes and perceptions of people and groups. This medium, though, can be incredibly variable among cultures. It is little wonder that groups of people who live in, use and value common "mundane phenomena of the material world", and yet perceive them through sometimes fundamentally different media, can come into direct conflict.

Problem Context

A large portion of the considerable body of work on environmental attitudes and perceptions in the Third World is found in international development literature. Hoben (1995), for example, traces the failure of many development initiatives to the fact that they are based on internationally accepted "development narratives" (an example would be the "tragedy of the commons" narrative) which are, in fact, culturally constructed and embedded in western development discourse. These narratives, he argues, all too often direct environmental policy and programs in developing countries, despite the fact that they frequently have little currency in local situations. The understanding of cultural variations in perceptions of the world, then, is crucial to the success of many international development undertakings.

Increasingly, the relevance of these issues to research concerned with indigenous populations is also being recognized. The academic attention focused on environmental attitudes and perceptions in the "Fourth World" owes its growing prominence not only to the practical need for conflict avoidance in the resource management community, but also to changing world politics and to trends in social and post-colonial theory. Clearly, much of this literature has been produced in response to the urgent call for co-operation between First Nations and dominant cultures in resource management, land claim, and energy and mining development contexts (Stoffle and Evans, 1990; Jorgensen, 1984). In other words, there is an immediate concern that exploitation and misunderstanding be avoided or, in many cases, mitigated.

Informing this obvious need for a greater understanding of First Nations' conceptions of landscape and nature, though, are the more intangible issues of historic and future justice. There is growing international consensus on the moral imperative for a recognition of indigenous rights to land and sovereignty (Klein, 1994, p. 1). This recognition must be facilitated by cross- and intra-cultural investigation which examines the various cultural understandings of even the most basic western concepts. The profound implications – economic, cultural and ecological – of differing cultural constructions of resource and environment underline the immediate need for a mutual understanding of those differences.

TOURISM

An emerging body of literature on environmental perceptions and attitudes in natural resource management situations deals with the increasingly important phenomenon of Third World tourism –including ecotourism –which is often seen almost as a panacea to the development ills of countries facing, in Mansfeld's (1992, p. 377) words, "an urgent need to overcome major economic and social problems, such as balance-of-payments deficits, heavy foreign debt, and high unemployment and urbanization rates" . Indeed, tourism has been touted in the development literature as a promising, sustainable, non-destructive strategy for economic development (Farrell, 1992; Smith and Eadington, 1992; deKadt, 1992).

Because of the immediate need for development solutions, tourism can be promoted as part of a central government initiative without sufficient consideration of its implications on a local level (Mansfeld, 1992; King and Stewart, 1996). In South Africa, the development of a tourism policy is taking place within the context of the RDP (Reconstruction and Development Programme), and it is expected that increased tourism in the country will (in addition to curing economic ills) promote national and cultural pride and unity (DEAT, 1995).

Along with the body of literature promoting tourism as an effective development strategy, however, there has been corresponding work warning of the pitfalls of mismanaged tourism and offering case studies illustrating such problems as environmental degradation, conflict over scarce resources, loss of cultural identity and loss of local control over resources (Brohman, 1996; see also Lindberg, Enriquez, Sproul, 1996; Mansfeld and Ginosar, 1994; Greenwood, 1997). Such problems can be linked, at least in part, to a failure to understand and take into account cultural differences in resource and landscape perception (Jackson, 1993; King and Stewart, 1996).

South Africa is only one of many places in the world where the need for effective, sustainable and culturally sensitive tourism policy is immediate. A richer understanding of the differences in the ways that culturally distinct populations at tourist destinations perceive their environments – the very resources and landscapes on which successful, or even merely lucrative, tourism depends – is one requisite for the formation of such policy.

SOUTH AFRICA AND RURAL DEVELOPMENT PLANNING

Almost 40 years of apartheid policy, under which people of colour were systematically and violently denied often even the most basic of human rights, have left their mark on every aspect of South African life. Apartheid's legacy includes crises in the fields of education, housing, employment and environment (IDRC, 1994). More basically, apartheid has left behind a society infused with the intolerance, factionalism, misunderstanding, hatred and psychological violence of racism. The psychological, attitudinal and behavioural aftermath of apartheid, then, provides both the most broad and the most fundamental context for this research.

After the 1994 democratic election in South Africa, the new African National Congress government, led by Nelson Mandela, set about the mammoth task of mounting a national reconstruction and development programme (RDP), which influences environmental, planning, social and tourism policy in the country. In addition, the RDP's overarching mission is to improve the quality of life for the country's citizens through economic growth and the redistribution of wealth (IDRC, 1994). The goals of the program, which are of particular significance for the research problem at Struis Bay, include the following:

- to ensure equitable access to natural resources;
- to improve access to marine resources for impoverished coastal communities;
- to provide safe and healthy living and working environments;
- to provide supportive measures to expand the small and micro-enterprise sector;
- to expand tourism and to integrate it into local development programmes.

TOURISM IN SOUTH AFRICA

In the RDP, tourism development, redistribution of wealth and environmental conservation are seen to be complementary rather than mutually exclusive goals. In addition, the advancement of tourism figures large in the RDP because of its supposed capacity to "promote nation-building and peace amongst the people of southern Africa as well as internationally", and to "create wealth, earn foreign exchange, and improve the quality of life for all South Africans" (DEAT, 1995, p. 14-15).

South African tourism policy is currently under review by the South African Department of Environmental Affairs and Tourism which, in 1995, published a working paper on the subject. In this "Green Paper", the South African Tourism

Council (SATC) was proposed as a multi-stakeholder body answerable to the Minister of Tourism, and responsible for the formulation and implementation of national tourism policy. The Green Paper is heavily infused with the sentiments of the RDP and is enthusiastically supportive of rapid international and domestic tourism development for the country. It recognizes that policy-makers must be cognizant of the potential pitfalls of tourism development, such as uneven and inequitable distribution of economic benefit, environmental degradation, leakage of benefits to remote or foreign agencies, and cultural or community exploitation (DEAT, 1995).

THE SOUTH AFRICAN FISHERY

Concurrent with these efforts to expand tourism in the country are attempts to ensure fair and equitable access to resources, including the fisheries. Such concerns have been incorporated into the broad administrative and research mandate of the South African Sea Fisheries Research Institute. Operating under the auspices of the Department of Environmental Affairs and Tourism, the agency is responsible for issuing commercial (or "A") and semi-commercial (or "B") fishing licences, for setting catch restrictions, and for the maintenance of the National Marine Line-fish System which is a database of catch and effort data and general line-fishery information.

THE STUDY SITE: STRUIS BAY, SOUTH AFRICA

The town of Struis Bay is located near Cape Agulhas, on the southernmost tip of the African continent, some 210 km southeast of Cape Town. The region enjoys a Mediterranean climate with mild winter rainfall and dry, windy summers. Moderated by the surrounding seas, temperatures in the Struis Bay area fluctuate from 7-18 degrees centigrade in the winter to 15-28 degrees in the summer (Burger, 1996; http/africa.com, 1997; http/africanet, 1997).

No authoritative history of the town of Struis Bay has been compiled, but there is evidence that it has supported a commercial fishery for at least the last century and a recreational fishing industry since the early part of the twentieth century. Before the 1960s, Struis Bay was a fishing village of approximately forty coloured families who lived in the immediate harbour area on land rented from a local white family. During the first half of this century, abundant game fish attracted anglers to the region and though the neighbouring town of L'Agulhas provided some services to these visiting fishers, the area supported only a small-scale tourist industry.

The National Party's efforts to legislate racial segregation in the country, embodied in the 1950 Group Areas Act, seem to have had delayed effects in Struis Bay. It was in 1960 that the act was used to declare the harbour area as "white-only", and the existing coloured community was relocated to an area some four kilometres from the harbour (Figure 6.1). This small new community was dubbed "Molshoop", or "Mole Heap", and its population has since grown to about 3000 permanent coloured residents.

Figure 6.1 Apartheid Era map of the Struis Bay and Molshoop Area, indicating designated European (E) and Coloured (C) areas of coastline

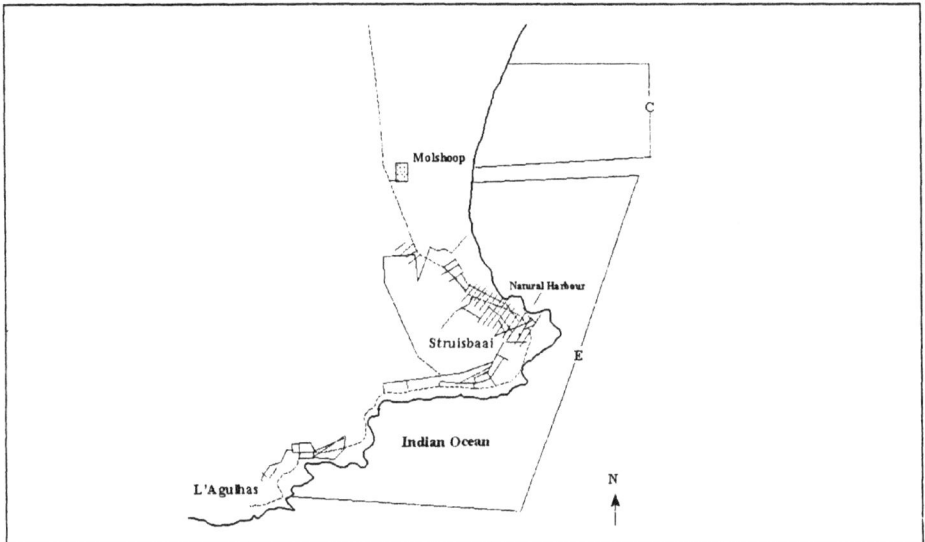

Source: Provided by Taylor, 1997. Personal communication. Original source unknown.

While tourism-related construction in the town has created some alternative employment for these people, most remain economically dependent on the commercial fishery. The overwhelming majority of fishers work for one of three local fishing companies who own the fishing fleets and to whom all fish must be sold.

The harbour area, meanwhile, was cleared of most of the previous residents' homes and was developed for white residential and business use. While the legislated geographical segregation of races in Struis Bay is a thing of the past, the town's coloured and white communities remain spatially and socially distinct. Molshoop, or Struis Bay North, is an exclusively non-white, low-income area, while Struis Bay proper is being actively promoted by a growing number of permanent white residents for further summer-home and tourist development. Opportunities for diving and the novelty of being at the southern tip of the continent attract some tourists to the area. Struis Bay's greatest drawing card, however, is its recreational line-fishing, an activity which is so popular in South Africa that annual investment therein is thought to exceed the annual wholesale value of all the country's marine resources put together (Manuel and Glazewski, 1991, p. 200).

RESEARCH DESIGN AND METHODOLOGY

Research approach: "writing ourselves in"

Herod's (1993) suggestion that, as researchers, we ought to be "writing ourselves into the research process" (p. 314) is a useful simplification of the directives emerging from hermeneutics. Starting with the basic presumption that "any investigation in social science needs to allow for the fact that social phenomena are not entirely external to the researcher" (Norton, 1989, p. 54), the hermeneutician seeks to acknowledge and theorize the representational role and positionality of the researcher with respect to the research subjects, thereby making explicit and productive that which has – in the positivist tradition – been either implicitly ignored or ostensibly controlled. In taking a hermeneutic approach, then, the researcher sought to acknowledge and articulate the role and position of the researchers at each stage of the investigative process, recognizing also that those roles and positions are not entirely subvertable. The researcher's hermeneutic task is, in effect, to attempt to make the research process transparent, thereby lending a greater degree of credibility to its products.

Choice of methodology

The choice of methodological approach for this project was guided by concerns as to how best to address the research problem and specific objectives, and was heavily informed by the theoretical approach outlined above. The in-depth interview was the primary methodology utilized, yielding data about the environmental perceptions of fishers. The suitability of the method for this research is outlined below. Participant-observation techniques, secondary sources and informant interviews yielded background and complementary data.

The in-depth interview method

The assumption underlying the in-depth interview is that detailed information about individuals' constructions and perceptions of a given reality, phenomenon or object are best expressed by that individual in his or her own language, form and context (i.e. rather than being expressed in imposed terms and selected fragments). However, there is, as Jones (1985, p. 47) argues, "no such thing as presuppositionless research". The proceedings are inevitably directed by the pre-ordained (however generally articulated) focus of the study and the lines of conversation deemed interesting or relevant by the researcher.

It is not the absence of direction, then, but the careful and restrained use of direction which is to be desired in an in-depth interview situation. It is for this reason that a *guided* in-depth interview method was selected; interviews took the form of informal and open conversations, but the interviewer's participation was directed by an interview guide which itemized important themes to be addressed in the exchange. Included in the guide were the following topics:

▶ Perceptions of the *resilience/renewability* of the resource;
▶ *Future use* (option demand) *value* of the resource for the benefit of future generations;
▶ *Non-use* (existence/intrinsic) *value* of the resource;
▶ Placement of the resource within a *culturally-determined value* system;
▶ Perceptions of *acceptable and inappropriate use* of the resource by various groups;
▶ Perception and opinions about past, current and future *relationships among fishing sectors,* including relationships of conflict or tension.

A number of characteristics of the in-depth interview method render it particularly appropriate in this research. These include: the adaptability to local and situational contingencies, allowing for the clarification of information and the establishment of trust; the depth, extent and subtlety of data yielded; the minimization of ambiguity in responses through the provision for elaboration on, and qualification of, what is said; and the explicitness of researcher intent and relative position.

Research time-line

Period of Time	Research Phase	Location
September 1996 to May 1997	Literature review; project development; correspondence with research partner	University of Guelph, Ontario, Canada
May, 1997	*Field Season I(a)* • orientation • collaboration with research partner • informant interviews • preparation for field work • refinement of interview guide	University of the Western Cape, Bellville, South Africa
June and July, 1997	*Field Season I(b)* *Focus Group: Local Commercial Fishers* • orientation in community • depth interviews • participation/observation • ongoing reflection	Struis Bay North (Molshoop), South Africa
July, 1997	*Field Season I(c)* • acquisition of secondary data • follow-up and closure	University of the Western Cape, Bellville, South Africa
August to November, 1997	Preliminary coding & analysis; follow up	University of Guelph, Ontario, Canada
November, 1997	*Field Season II(a)* • presentation of preliminary findings • preparation for field work • informant interviews	University of the Western Cape, Bellville, South Africa
November and December, 1997	*Field Season II(b)* • orientation in community • informant interviews • depth interviews • participation/observation • ongoing reflection	Struis Bay, South Africa
January to March, 1998, and ongoing	Data preparation, coding and analysis; write-up; dissemination of results	University of Guelph, Ontario, Canada

FIELD SEASON ONE

Preparation and informant interviews

The period from May 15 to June 1997 was spent working out of the Department of Earth Sciences at the University of the Western Cape in Bellville, a suburb of Cape Town. At this time, the main research tasks were *(a)* the arrangement of informant interviews, *(b)* the preparation for and logistical organization of the coming days in the field, and *(c)* the refinement and editing of the in-depth interview guide, based in part on the results of informant interviews.

The purpose of the interviews was to gain anecdotal background information on the nature and extent of past and current conflict among fishery user groups in the study area, and about the general conditions in the town. It was hoped that, through these conversations, the interviewer would be able to identify issues around which controversy has centred, and to hear from individuals with diverse political, racial and institutional affiliations. In total, six interviews were conducted with a range of respondents, including a biologist at Cape Town's oceanarium and a zoologist at the University of the Western Cape, an African National Congress Member of Parliament and a local ANC promoter and organizer in Molshoop, administrators at the South African Sea Fisheries Research Institute in Cape Town, and a co-owner of a small Struis Bay fish buying company.

The informant interviews deepened the researcher's understanding of the context from which the fishers would be responding. This understanding, then, strongly informed the concurrent refinement of the in-depth interview guide, including the formulation of possible modes of questioning for the subsequent in-depth interview process.

In-depth interviews, participant observation and ongoing reflection

The period from June 9 to July 20, 1997 was spent living in Struis Bay North, or "Molshoop", where the majority of permanent coloured residents of Struis Bay reside. During this time the principal tasks were to:

- become familiar with the community and to inform community members of the purpose of the visit;
- to undertake in-depth interviews with the help of a translator;
- to observe and, where possible, to participate in the life of the community.

The second of these tasks – arranging in-depth interviews – was at once the most important and the most challenging. As anticipated, the differences in race, nationality, gender and level of education between the researcher and interview respondents represented partial barriers to immediate effective communication. An initial period of adjustment and ongoing casual interaction with community members was needed to build relationships of trust with individuals and for residents to become accustomed to the presence of the researcher before interviewing could properly begin.

During the field season fifteen interviews, ranging in length from one to three hours each, were conducted with commercial fishers in the community, who responded almost exclusively in Afrikaans. The conversations took place in the respondents' homes and were recorded on micro-cassette. Interviews were arranged by direct contact with people at the harbour and in Molshoop or by a "snowball" method, whereby one respondent suggests others who may be interested in responding. Notes describing the tone and dynamic of the conversation, the extra-interview activity that took place, and non-verbal communication that occurred were taken immediately following each interview, when possible. Subsequent to this, the interviews themselves were transcribed into English from the tapes.

The method of participant observation was used to provide background and context for the interview results. In addition to the inevitable daily casual interactions with individuals in Molshoop, specific community events or activities in which the researcher was able to participate, or which she could observe, provided insight about the shared "life world" of fishers and their larger cultural sphere in Struis Bay North (Table 6.1). On such occasions detailed field notes and – where possible and appropriate – photos served as records of the events and the researcher's role in them.

Because this study was grounded in the principles of hermeneutics, it was deemed important for the researcher to engage in ongoing consideration and interrogation of her role in each methodological process and how her position as a researcher and an individual was affecting the outcomes of those processes. To this end, the researcher kept a regular journal of reflections on these subjects and on the progress of the research itself throughout the time spent in Struis Bay North.

Table 6.1 Field Season One: Instances of participation in and/or observation of community life by the researcher

Event/Interaction	Date	Description of Participation
Day at Sea	June 20, 1997	Accompanied an eight-man commercial crew on a typical day of fishing out of the Struis Bay harbour.
Family Visit	June 20, 1997	Accompanied a local commercial fisher, his wife and grand-daughter on a visit to see relations in a neighbouring fishing village.
'Tour' of Struis Bay	June 22, 1997	Accompanied a commercial fisherman and prominent community member on a driving 'tour' of the town, during which pre-relocation landmarks were identified and described (e.g. where old houses had stood, where defunct cemeteries lie, etc.).
Extended Conversation	June 27, 1997	Participated in a long, casual conversation with two local commercial fishers in one of the men's home.
Extended Conversation	June 27, 1997	Participated in a long, casual conversation with a non-fishing couple in the community.
Church Service	June 28, 1997	Attended a local Anglican morning worship service in Molshoop.
Extended Conversation	July 6, 1997	Participated in a long, casual conversation with a local white businesswoman and a few of her clients and associates.
Day at Sea	July 11, 1997	Again accompanied an eight-man commercial crew on a typical day of fishing out of Struis Bay harbour.
Extended Conversation	July 12, 1997	Participated in a long, casual conversation with a local commercial fisher.

Secondary data

A considerable amount of secondary data was kindly provided by the South African Sea Fisheries Research Institute, based in Cape Town. These data included:

▶ Reports and articles describing the past and present state of fish stocks in the Struis Bay area;

▶ Catch and Effort data for licenced fishers in the Struis Bay area;

▶ Documentation of current licencing policy, and of both commercial and recreational fishing rules and restrictions which apply to Struis Bay fishers.

FIELD SEASON TWO

The second season in the field followed roughly the same pattern as that outlined above for field season one. Since the focus group for this second season was the recreational fishing community (many members of which are seasonal visitors to Struis Bay), it was necessary to conduct the research during the summer months when tourism is at a peak and the targeted line-fish are most plentiful.

Preparation and informant interviews

As was the case during the previous field season, the most important initial tasks were the arrangement of informant interviews and the further development of the interview guide based on those responses. Respondents in the four informant interviews which were conducted included representatives of the Struis Bay Deep Sea Angling Club and of the South African Deep Sea Fishing Association, the owner of a prosperous local fish buying company, and a prominent member of the Struis Bay recreational fishing community.

In-depth interviews, participant observation and ongoing reflection

During the period from November 25, 1997 to January 7, 1998 a language translator and the researcher lived in the Struis Bay municipal caravan park and undertook seventeen in-depth interviews with recreational fishers. These interviews were conducted primarily in English at the respondents' homes and were from one to three hours in length. Also during this time, the researcher was able to participate in various meetings and events held by individuals or groups in the recreational fishing community, and these experiences were again recorded in the form of notes and, occasionally, photos (Table 6.2).

Table 6.2 Field Season Two: Instances of participation in and/or observation of community life by the researcher

Event/ Interaction	Date	Description of Participation
Extended Conversation	November 27, 1997	Participated in a long, casual conversation with a prominent white community member, who is a commercial fisher, a recreational fisher and the proprietor of a small fishing excursion business.
Meeting of the Struis Bay Sea Angling Club	December 4, 1997	Attended a meeting/social night of the local Sea Angling Club (SBSAC)
Social Visit	December 9, 1997	Attended a Barbeque dinner party hosted by a visiting recreational angler.
Meeting of the SBSAC	December 11, 1997	Attended a second meeting/social night of the local Sea Angling Club.
Annual General Meeting	December 18, 1997	Attended the Annual General Meeting of the local Sea Angling Club.
Extended Conversation	January 4, 1998	Participated in a long, casual conversation with the (white) proprietor of a local fish buying company and owner of a local fleet of fishing boats.

Data analysis

In designing an interview schedule or guide, the challenge is to strike a balance between over-directiveness and extreme vagueness. The process of analyzing interview data, not surprisingly, demanded a similar balancing act. Analysis, of necessity, involved the imposition of structure and organization onto the set of data. The imposition of culturally inappropriate, overly academic or personally biased constructs onto the data, however, was clearly to be avoided. Nonetheless, it is inevitable that the researcher will to some degree impose (however self-consciously and explicitly) her or his own interpretive framework onto the data. In this study, this framework took the form of the preordained thematic organization of the conversations in the interview guide. To some other degree, however, structure and meaning must have their generation *in the data themselves* in order to maintain a standard of fidelity to the real concerns and perceptions of the people about (not to say *for*) whom they are supposed to speak.

The analysis of the in-depth interview transcripts sought to recognize broad trends and patterns of similarity or difference in perceptions of the resource both within and among user groups. Data were then fragmented into meaningful units ranging from one sentence to a small paragraph, and coded or classified thematically. These categories were analysed for links among them and sub-categories within them, and ultimately broad trends in the focus groups' environmental perceptions were identified and described. Finally, it should be noted that interrogation and testing of theories occurred on an ongoing basis to reduce the likelihood of misguided or imposed ideas becoming entrenched in the analysis.

It was only after the interview data had been analyzed on their own that background data collected by means of participant observation and from secondary sources was applied to the further interpretation of transcripts. At this point, links and/or incongruencies among perceptions, resource use and points of conflict were identified. In addition, the introduction of background data prompted a search for patterns not previously identified in the in-depth interview data. It was at this final stage that the full data set was considered in the formulation of guidelines for effective tourism and development policy in Struis Bay.

RESULTS

Focus group one: full-time commercial fishers

All of the 15 commercial fishers interviewed were coloured men between the ages of 30 and 80 who relied on fishing as their primary source of income. Only one respondent owned a boat; most Molshoop fishers are crew-members or skippers on boats owned by the local fishing companies. All of these boats are licenced for commercial fishing and those who fish from them must fish according to the "A" licence's requirements, including size restrictions and bag limits. The one respondent who owned his own boat, however, held a "B" (semi-commercial) licence and was therefore subject to slightly more strict bag limits.

Three orders of codes were developed in order to identify a segment of text according to (a) the phenomenon it literally described or to which it referred (e.g. the moral character of youth in the community), (b) the generic but recurring theme to which it indirectly spoke (e.g. the nostalgic comparison of past with present conditions or behaviours), and (c) the broad pattern in the data of which it seems to be a part (e.g. an apparent alienation from the ways and values of the emerging generation of fishers). This final, most developed, code order – the pattern codes – formed the basis for a preliminary attempt at schematizing the results (Figure 6.2).

Figure 6.2 Preliminary schematic diagram illustrating apparent links among pattern codes for depth interview data. Focus group: Commercial fishers, Struis Bay North, South Africa

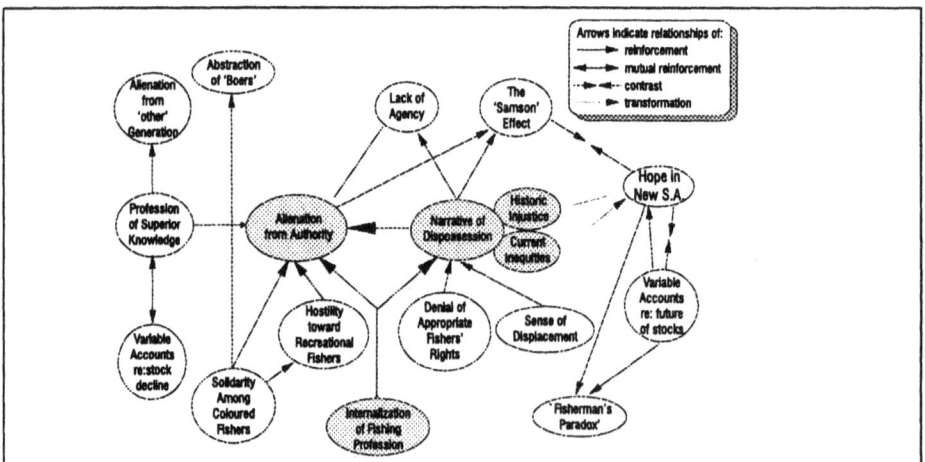

It was apparent from the interview data that a perceived pattern of historical and ongoing injustice – which centred in many interviews around the story of the 1960 community relocation and which took the more general form of a narrative of dispossession – deeply informed the fishers' perceptions of the fishery, their role in the industry, the future of the profession and the behaviour of recreational fishers. Most clearly, this shared sense of having been wronged, which seemed almost to have had the effect of creating a culture of oppression, has apparently caused a fundamental alienation from actual or perceived authority and power. This alienation, in turn, posed problems for the fishers' understanding and acceptance of externally imposed fishing rules and regulations.

Connected to these themes was the deeply felt and consistently expressed rift among racial groups – a pervasive and generalizing "us-versus-them" mentality which is hardly surprising in the aftermath of apartheid – which underlay much of the tension and animosity between commercial fishers and other groups, including recreational fishers, fishing policy administrators and local fish buying companies. This group identification as "us", of course, encompassed not only race but also profession. Thus, the meaning of what it is to be a coloured person in Struis Bay was bound up with what it is to be a commercial fisher in that place; this is where the fishers' perceptions of the fishery resource itself and their felt sense of dispossession intersected. It would seem that the fishery was seen both as a birthright and as yet another tool of oppression.

Finally, there was an apparent perception among commercial fishers that the conditions under which they live and work, and the economic and natural system of which they are a part, are entirely outside of their control either because they have been naturalized as "just the way it is" or because the reigns of power are seen to be so firmly held in other (white) hands. Not unexpectedly, this lack of agency seemed to spring from an actual historical lack of power and appeared to be exacerbated by current social conditions in the community such as low income and education and widespread alcoholism.

Focus group two: recreational fishers

Recreational fishers in Struis Bay represent a more diverse group than commercial fishers. Recreational fishers may be residents (usually retired) or visitors and they may fish strictly for sport (classified here as "recreational-casual") or they may hold a "B" licence, allowing them to fish commercially when they choose, albeit with restrictions (classified here as "recreational-commercial"). Virtually all recreational fishers in this area – and all respondents in this study – are white, middle-class males.

In total, 17 interviews were conducted with fishers between the ages of 23 and 65. In all cases, the respondents said their primary motive for fishing was pleasure or sport and they did not rely on fishing for an essential source of income. All interviewees were either otherwise employed or retired. Of the 17 fishers interviewed, 13 owned their own outboard-motor boats. Eleven of these boat owners held a "B", or semi-commercial licences, and the remaining six respondents admitted to illegally selling fish on a small scale.

Not surprisingly, the interviews conducted with recreational fishers seemed to centre around many of the same themes which figured prominently in conversations with commercial fishers. At this stage, three principle themes have emerged from the data: the impact of apartheid's legacy on the perceptions of members of this white community; the perceptions of territory and fishing rights, and how they are justified; and the discussion of the fish stocks themselves, the resource's resilience, and how it is to be conserved.

Firstly, it comes as no shock that apartheid has left its mark in white as well as non-white communities. In this case, the divisions among racial and cultural groups which were exaggerated and legislated under apartheid persist in the ways that group identification is articulated. Recreational fishers' self-identity as "white" and as "Afrikaaner" seemed to converge with that as "fisherman" and "sportsman". The virtues and characteristics ascribed to the avid sportsman (e.g. responsibility, dedication, competitive spirit), then, were often seen to overlap with traditional white and Afrikaaner qualities. Again, race is seen to be a principle factor in distinguishing between self and other, and the deeply felt, long-standing racial divisions in Struis Bay seem to largely dictate the nature of relationships among sub-groups in the community and perceptions of how and by whom the resource ought to be managed.

In addition, there is a general indication in the interview data that the end of the apartheid era has engendered feelings of disempowerment and vulnerability in the "new" South Africa. Connected to this is an oft-expressed hostility towards the ANC government both in general terms and more specifically as a result of the perceived mismanagement of the fishery resource. During interviews, the fact that administrative power has been transferred from white to black or coloured hands was repeatedly cited as a reason for individuals' lack of confidence in government agencies managing the fishery.

Secondly, there was a strong sense in these conversations that the sea and harbour are often sites where territory and rights to the resource are negotiated. While recreational fishers claimed a natural right to access to the sea – a South African's birthright – there was a perception that it was by virtue of their boat and property ownership, their regular payment for harbour facilities, and their personal involvement in conservation practices that they ought to be allocated continued and enhanced fishing rights.

Finally, there is an evident perception among recreational fishers that the fishery has generally been mismanaged, particularly since the fall of apartheid. Individuals' personal sense of environmental stewardship and fishing ethics (the practice of following conservation regulations and catch restrictions, for example) was frequently described as better developed than that of commercial fishers, in addition to being cited as a justification for continued access to the sea. Many expressed real concern over the future of the stocks. It should be noted that while there was bitterness about the local commercial fishers' perceived irresponsibility vis-à-vis conservation practices, the serious damage to fish stocks was attributed to large off-shore trawlers, rather than to local commercial enterprises.

OUTPUTS AND CONTRIBUTIONS OF THE RESEARCH

Practical significance

This research comes at a time in South Africa's history when there is an immediate need for equitable and effective tourism and fishery policy which is applicable at a local level. These policy concerns are, moreover, intimately tied to the need for community development in South Africa which focuses on healing, reconciliation and mutual understanding. It is hoped that the policy guidelines and recommendations emerging from the study at Struis Bay will have practical relevance to policy development, which would take appropriate account of the importance of cultural and sub-cultural differences in resource perceptions at tourist destinations.

It is evident that in Struis Bay deeply-rooted cultural and racial divisions among fishing sectors have given rise to divergent opinions about the way the resource ought to be managed, perceptions of the appropriate use of the resource, and ways of participating in its exploitation. By clarifying some of these differences, identifying issues of importance to fishers and tracing the sources of contention, the research can enrich the information base on which policy-makers in the region might draw. This understanding of the stakeholders' perceptions is key to a productive dialogue between sectors and the effective communication among fishers, other community members, administrators and researchers on which successful fishing and tourism policy depends.

Struis Bay, though, is not alone in facing the challenges (and reaping the benefits) that rapid tourism development brings. There is considerable potential for marine resource-based tourism in countless similar communities on South Africa's coast. It is therefore anticipated that the information and guidelines emerging from this study will be relevant – in an adapted form – to tourism policy change and/or the expansion of ecotourism outside of the Struis Bay region.

Methodological and theoretical contributions

Because of the highly pliable and adaptable nature of the in-depth interview method, the specifics of its use – the interview style and structure, the approach to data organization and analysis – are unique to each research endeavor in which it is employed. For this reason, every new study using the method becomes an important resource for subsequent researchers considering its application. This study will thus contribute to such a resource base for future investigators.

Finally, it is hoped and expected that this study will contribute to the current knowledge about and understanding of the "cultural factor" – particularly as it relates to perceptions of resources – in situations of conflict. This understanding is crucial to the just and effective resolution of such conflicts in all parts of the world. In addition – while the research does not test a given theory of culture or of landscape perceptions – insofar as it documents and analyzes cultural difference in resource perception, it will nonetheless have a theoretical contribution to make to the field.

ENDNOTES

1. Under the Apartheid system in South Africa, individuals were classified according to an imposed system of racial categories including Black (indigenous, or tribal African), Asian (largely Indian), Coloured (of 'mixed race'), and White, or European. While this terminology rings – at least in North American ears – of the racism of the regime responsible for its formulation, it largely persists in Post-Apartheid South Africa. In this chapter, the term 'coloured' will be used to

describe those who were classified as such under the previous governmen *because this continues to be the self-designation of people in that group;* I will refer to people in the terms in which they describe themselves.

REFERENCES

Africanet. 1997: *South Africa.* www.africanet/country/s.africa.htp

Africa. 1997: *South Africa.* www.africa.com/captour/captour.htm

Attwood, C.G. and Bennett, B.A. 1995: A Procedure for Setting Daily Bag Limits on the Recreational Shore-Fishery of the South-Western Cape, *South Africa. South African Journal of Marine Science,* 15, 241-251.

Brohman, J. 1996: New Directions in Tourism for Third World Development. *Annals of Tourism Research,* 23 (1), 48-70.

Burdge, R.J. 1996: Introduction: Cultural Diversity in Natural Resource Use. *Society and Natural Resources,* 9 (1-2), 1-2.

Burger, D. (ed.). 1996: *South Africa Yearbook.* Cape Town: CTP Book Printers.

DEAT. 1995: *Tourism Green Paper: Towards a New Tourism Policy for South Africa.* Pretoria: Department of Environmental Affairs and Tourism, South Africa.

deKadt, E. 1992: Making the Alternative Sustainable. Lessons for Development in Tourism. In V. Smith and W. Eadington (eds.), *Tourism Alternatives: Potentials and Problems in the Development of Tourism,* pp. 47-75. Philadelphia: University of Pennsylvania Press.

Edelstein, M.R. and Kleese, D.A. 1995: Cultural Relativity of Impact Assessment: Native Hawaiian Opposition to Geothermal Energy Development. *Society and Natural Resources,* 8 (1), 19- 31.

Farrell, B. 1992: Tourism as an Element in Sustainable Development: Hana, Maui. In V. Smith and W. Eadington (eds.), *Tourism Alternatives: Potentials and Problems in the Development of Tourism,* pp. 115-134. Philadelphia: University of Pennsylvania Press.

Greenwood, D. 1997: Culture by the pound: an anthropological perspective on tourism as cultural commoditization. In V. Smith (ed.), *Hosts and Guests: the Anthropology of Tourism,* pp. 171-186. Philadelphia: University of Pennsylvania Press.

Herod, A. 1993: Gender issues in the use of interviewing as a research method. *Professional Geographer,* 45 (3), 305-317.

Hoben, A. 1995: Paradigms and Politics: The Cultural Construction of Environmental policy in Ethiopia. *World Development,* 23 (6), 1007-1021.

IDRC. 1994: *Environment, Reconstruction and Development in the New South Africa.* Johannesburg: IDRC/ANC/COSATU/SACP/SANCO Mission on Environmental Policy.

Jackson, P. 1980: A plea for cultural geography. *Area,* 12 (1), 110-113.

Jackson, P. 1989: *Maps of Meaning.* Boston: Unwin Hyman.

Jackson, P. 1993: Changing Ourselves: A Geography of Position. In R.J. Johnston (ed.), *The Challenge for Geography, A Changing World: A Changing Discipline,* pp. 198-214. Oxford: Blackwell.

Jones, S. 1985: Depth Interviewing. In R. Walker (ed.), *Applied Qualitative Research,* pp. 45-55. Brookfield: Gower.

Jorgensen, J.G. 1984: Commentary: Native Americans and Rural Anglos: Conflicts and Cultural Responses to Energy Developments. *Human Organization,* 43 (2), 178-185.

King, D. and Stewart, W.P. 1996: Ecotourism and Commodification: protecting people and places. *Biodiversity and Conservation,* 5 (3), 293-305.

Klein, D. 1994: Wilderness: A Western Concept Alien to Arctic Cultures. *Information North,* 20 (3), 1-6.

Lindberg, K., Enriquez, J. and Sproul, K. 1996: Ecotourism Questioned: Case Studies from Belize. *Annals of Tourism Research,* 23 (3), 543-562.

Mansfeld, Y. 1992: Group-differentiated Perceptions of Social Impacts Related to Tourism Development. *Professional Geographer,* 44 (4), 377-392.

Mansfeld, Y. and Ginosar, O. 1994: Evaluation of the Repertory Grid Method in Studies of Locals' Attitude towards Tourism Development Processes. *Environment and Planning,* A, 26 (6), 957-972.

Manuel, F. and Glazewski, J. 1991: The Oceans: Our Common Heritage. In J. Cock and E. Kock (eds.), *Going Green: People, Politics, and the Environment in South Africa,* pp. 193-209. Cape Town: Oxford University Press.

Norton, W. 1989: *Explorations in the Understanding of Landscape: a Cultural Geography.* New York: Greenwood Press.

Smith, V. and Eadington, W. (eds.). 1992: *Tourism Alternatives.* Philadelphia: University of Pennsylvania.

Stoffle, R.W. and Evans, M.J. 1990: Holistic Conservation and Cultural Triage: American Indian Perspectives on Cultural Resources. *Human Organization,* 49 (2), 91-99.

Zelinsky, W. 1992: *The Cultural Geography of the United States.* New Jersey: Prentice Hall.

Chapter 7

An Environmental Impact Assessment of Tourism in Zambia's Lower Zambezi National Park

by Excellent Hachileka

Introduction

This chapter reports on a study conducted in the Lower Zambezi National Park in Zambia. The study assessed the environmental impacts of the increasing numbers of tourists visiting the park.

Tourism is the world's fastest growing industry and employs millions of people. In Zambia, it is one of the major earners of foreign exchange. Zambia's tourism industry is largely based on the country's large wildlife areas, which cover about 30% of the country. Other tourist attractions include spectacular landscapes such as Victoria Falls and a diversity of rich cultures and history.

The Lower Zambezi National Park is one of the relatively undisturbed wildlife sanctuaries in the southern African region. The park's tourist attractions include abundant wildlife, the mighty Zambezi River, and diverse ecosystems and habitats which support a wide variety of large mammals, birds, fish and insects.

Tourism is said to be transforming the world's natural beauty into an economic commodity, comparable in value to gold or diamonds. In the process, the tourism industry has planted seeds of self-destruction in that the more tourism succeeds, the more it cannibalizes the very basis of its existence.

In many parts of the world where nature's beauty has been harnessed and packaged for tourism, there is now concern about a variety of perceived and actual environmental and socio-economic impacts. Wilderness areas are being severely damaged by uncontrolled and unregulated tourist use.

Where tourism is developed without planning for conserving and protecting the resources upon which they are based, negative environmental and socio-economic impacts may result.

Environmental impacts of tourism are associated with three main components of the industry: transport and travel infrastructure, construction of accommodation and shelter, and recreational activities. The actual impacts are related to the increasing number of visitors and vehicles coming to an area, frequency and intensity of use of certain areas, and the type of tourist activities involved (Buckely and Pannell, 1990).

The impacts most likely caused by tourism developments are vegetation disturbance through clearing and vehicle and pedestrian traffic; soil erosion and sedimentation of surface water run-off; solid waste disposal; water pollution; wildlife disturbance and habitat destruction; noise and intrusive visual impressions (DCEC, 1993).

For communities in destination areas, the many consequences of tourism development may be positive or negative. Interaction between the local community and the tourists varies with the cultural distance between the indigenous people and the tourists (Matheison and Wall, 1982). While this interaction may put pressure on available resources and facilities, it can provide positive effects such as economic benefit through employment creation, produce market opportunities, and use of tourist facilities by the local communities.

More often than not, however, the differences between the local community and the visitors cause negative results such as behaviour or dress which is offensive to the local culture, smoking, prostitution and begging. Contact between the local community and visitors can lead to cultural erosion, especially when traditional values and indigenous practices are turned into tourist attractions. Tours of archaeological sites are often pursued against the local traditional or religious beliefs (World Bank, 1991).

Good environmental planning and management are particularly crucial in nature-based tourism because, unlike other industries, nature-based tourism is inherently a danger to itself. Its success increases the likelihood of negative environmental impact and degradation of the very attraction which draws visitors.

However, if well planned and managed, nature tourism has the potential for low environmental impact with high and sustainable economic returns. It is important that environmental concerns are made an integral part of tourism development planning to avoid or minimize any potentially negative impacts.

In Zambia, the National Environmental Action Plan has developed some strategies to minimize and ultimately prevent unnecessary negative effects of tourism development on the environment:

▶ All major tourist development activities are subject to environmental impact assessments;

▶ In protected areas, only tourism development which conforms to management plans for the area will be approved;

▶ A data bank of accurate statistics will be compiled for use in the planning of medium- and long-term tourism development.

The Environmental Protection and Pollution Control Act No. 12 of 1990 is Zambia's principal environmental legislation. It led to the creation of the Environmental Council of Zambia (ECZ), a regulatory and enforcement body responsible for coordinating environmental activities of all government ministries and other bodies concerned with environmental protection. The Act covers air, water, waste disposal, pesticide use, toxic substance control, noise, ionizing radiation and natural resources conservation. A number of regulations for control of these environmental issues are already in place. These include the Environmental Impact Assessment Regulations of 1997 (EPPCA, 1990), which outline the procedures and requirements for environmental impact assessment (EIA) in Zambia. The ECZ is mandated to identify projects, programs, plans and policies that may require an EIA. Developers are compelled to undertake EIA studies where they are deemed necessary by the ECZ. Regulations require EIA studies for tourism enterprises to be established in national parks and wetland areas.

This has been a welcome development because project proposals, plans and programs in the past have not benefited from any degree of environmental planning associated with EIAs. This has obviously had negative implications for natural systems and socio-economic environments. With the introduction of EIA regulations, project decisions are no longer based solely on economic considerations, but take into account principles and objectives based on environmental maintenance and enhancement.

These policies are based on the realization that tourism potential lies in the uniqueness of resources such as wildlife, landscapes and cultural artifacts (Muliya, 1997) and an understanding that these resources must be safeguarded for future generations.

Investment in Zambia's tourism industry during the 1990s has been phenomenal. It is important that this investment be supported by proper tourism development planning to minimize and prevent undesirable effects on tourist attractions and the environment. Unfortunately, as in most countries, Zambia's research on tourism has tended to emphasize economic impacts at the expense of social and environmental impacts.

Aware of the threat of environmental degradation associated with tourism development, the Department of National Parks and Wildlife Services (NPWS), the executive arm of the government responsible for implementing the wildlife policy and legislation, commissioned the development of a management plan for Lower Zambezi National Park. The objective was to draw up comprehensive plans for the conservation of the park's bio-diversity and the development of a sustainable tourism industry.

The Lower Zambezi National Park Management Plan was completed in 1992. It called for dividing the park into four separate areas, namely: conservation, wild, wilderness and development zones.

In the development zone, the plan recommended a total of 11 tourist accommodation development sites, including the existing ones. Unfortunately, the management plan did not fully address the environmental impacts of the tourism development envisaged. Many aspects of the proposed development which should have been included were not assessed to determine the environmental impacts and required mitigation measures. This assessment was particularly critical, given that the Lower Zambezi is such an ecologically fragile site.

Upon NPWS approval of the Lower Zambezi National Park Management Plan, development commenced on nine of the eleven sites identified for a five-year lease. To date, nine tourist lodges have been established and are operating without any comprehensive environmental management strategy for minimizing the likely environmental impacts of the lodges, the associated infrastructure and park activities. It was inevitable that a full-scale environmental impact assessment of tourism development in the park would need to be undertaken to secure the sustainability of the tourism industry in the area.

This chapter presents the results of a study which attempted to close the gaps in the 1992 Lower Zambezi National Park Management Plan. The study examined the environmental aspects of tourism development which had not been fully considered previously. The study assessed tourist impacts on the environment by gathering information on facilities, visitor numbers and tourist activities, on one hand, and the potential impacts of interaction between visitors and the area's particular types of ecosystems and habitats, on the other.

The study was conducted late in the planning cycle, when the decision had already been made to proceed with tourism development in the area. It was important to identify all the mitigation measures and management strategies needed to safeguard the environment from degradation resulting from the existing tourism enterprise in the park. This assessment focuses on measures to control the potential impacts resulting from greater use of the infrastructure and natural areas of the park.

To achieve the study's general objective, a set of research activities were developed:

▶ to identify the existing tourist resources and recreation activities in the Lower Zambezi National Park;

▶ to identify the significant environmental and socio-economic impacts of tourism development in the park and the surrounding game management areas;

▶ to develop a mitigation plan for environmental and socio-economic impacts of tourism development in the park and the surrounding game management area.

The Study Area

The most recently gazetted of Zambia's 19 national parks, the Lower Zambezi National Park (LZNP) was declared by statutory instrument No. 38 of 1983. The park covers 4092 km² and is located 180 km southeast of Lusaka, the capital of Zambia. It lies between latitudes 15 degrees 7 minutes south and 15 degree 44 minutes south, longitude 29 degrees 10 minutes east and 30 degrees 10 minutes east. As Figure 7.1 shows, the LZNP lies along the north bank of the Zambezi River, with 120 km of river frontage. The park extends across two districts of Lusaka province, namely Lusaka rural and Luangwa.

Figure 7.1 Loaction of Lower Zambezi National Park

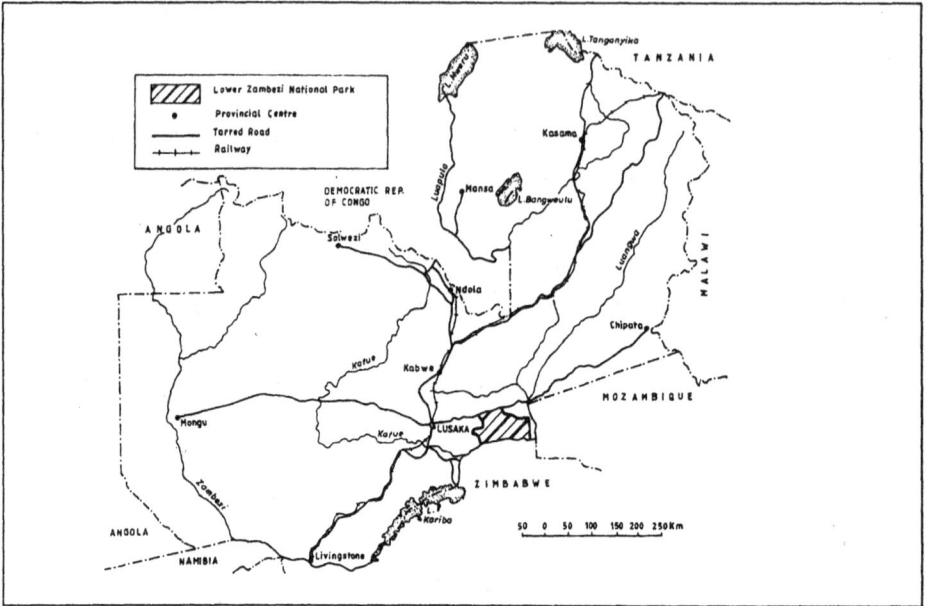

The area's tourist season extends from March to December. The park is generally accessible by land, air and water.

Land access is seasonally limited. There is little road infrastructure in the valley, as much of the area is uninhabited and very rugged terrain. The main road from Lusaka to Harare crosses the Zambezi at Chirundu. A minor road branches off from Chirundu, crossing the Kafue River by pontoon, continuing through Chieftainess Chiawa's area to the national park. The unimproved seasonal road passes through the park and joins the Luangwa road on the other side.

Air access is rarely used. The Jeki airstrip serves visitors to the park only in the dry season. With 120 km of frontage on the Zambezi River, the park is easily accessed by water.

The status of the park, in terms of its recognition as a protected area, dates back to 1951 when an area slightly smaller than the present park was declared as a first-class controlled hunting area. In 1973, the area was granted the status of an international park under the jurisdiction of Wildlife Conservation International (WCI), a consortium interested in developing the park. The consortium was funded by United States government foreign aid to Zambia, and the area was leased to this organization for a period of 25 years. However, WCI withdrew in 1974 because the area became unsafe due to the escalation of the Zimbabwean liberation war across the Zambezi River. The park was closed to safaris during the Rhodesia war and was Zambia's forgotten wilderness for many years. Following Zimbabwe's independence in 1981, the area was declared the Lower Zambezi National Park.

Much of the park lies in a valley which is an extension of the Great Rift Valley system. The region is one of the hottest and driest parts of Zambia, primarily because it is low-lying. The average altitude of the Lower Zambezi area is about 380-m a.s.l, as compared to the mean altitude of the rest of the country at 1,200-m a.s.l, so it tends to have a low-altitude climate which is not subject to the modifying effects of most of the country's plateau areas (University of Zambia, 1987).

The park experiences a continental tropical climate with three seasons. These may be distinguished as a hot rainy season from late November to April, a cool dry season from May to August, and a hot dry season from September to early November. Rainfall in this area is quite variable and unreliable. The mean annual rainfall ranges from 400 to 700mm. Evaporation is usually about three times as much as precipitation. The cool dry season from June to August is not as severe as on the plateau, while the hot dry season from September to November is notably hotter, with maximum temperatures in October ranging from 34 to 37 degrees celsius (NPWS, 1992).

The park is composed of three physiographic regions, namely, the plateau, the escarpment and the valley. The plateau area covers the northern part of the park, extending from the Nyamangwe and Chakwenga Rivers in the north to the road leading to the old Chakwenga mine. The plateau is characterized by a rolling topography of ridges and *dambos* dissected by small drainage lines. The altitude on the plateau ranges from 900 to 1300m (NPWS, 1992).

The escarpment is generally oriented in a northeast-southwest direction. It is composed of rugged topography with deeply dissected massive ridges of various heights, ranging on average from 750 to 1200m. The escarpment forms a complex divide of drainage systems flowing both east-west and north-south. The rugged nature of the ridges, dissected by numerous drainage lines, provides spectacular scenery, which is heightened by panoramic views over the valley floor and the Zambezi River (NPWS, 1992).

Two physiographic units are found in the valley floor area. These are a dissected trough floor and a flat trough. The dissected trough floor unit comprises areas of active deposition of colluvium from the escarpment, characterized by foot slopes, alluvial fans and many ephemeral streams. The streams flow only in the wet season, when they cause a lot of erosion. The flat trough floor comprises alluvial features such as river terraces and the flood plain which includes point bars, cut-off meanders, abandoned channels and back swamps (Dalal-Clayton, 1985).

The Zambezi River and ephemeral streams largely dominate the drainage of the Lower Zambezi National Park. Other rivers in the system include the Chongwe, Mushingiswa, Musangashi, Chakwenga, Mushika, Musensenshi, Chamitondo and Musupuli. These rivers and the Zambezi provide most of the water resources required for the fauna and flora in the park. These rivers flow until the end of the cool dry season, after which isolated pools remain in the escarpment and on the plateau (Sichingabula, 1997).

There are a number of springs in the escarpment and several *dambos* are found in the plateau and valley floor. These are common mainly in seasonally waterlogged grassland areas usually dissected by streams (Handlos and Haward, 1985).

The area has several vegetation types which are closely associated with the physiography, geology, soils and moisture regimes. The vegetation types are generally zoned along topographic gradients and more or less run parallel to the course of the Zambezi River. Within each physiographic zone, the variation in soil type has given rise to a mosaic of vegetation types, each with its own characteristic floristic composition. Five major vegetation types are found in the area: the miombo, mopane and munga woodlands, riparian forest and some grasslands.

This vegetation diversity in Lower Zambezi is important for it supports a diversity of species, including grazers and browsers. In fact, the habitat and food preferences shown by some animals is an indication of the numerous ecological niches. Numerous plant communities cater to a diversity of animals that exist in the valley.

The purpose of Lower Zambezi National Park is to conserve and protect the wildlife and Zambezi River valley ecosystem, the high bio-diversity of fauna and flora, the water catchment for the Zambezi River system and the area's cultural heritage. In addition, the park is meant to support scientific research, public education opportunities, and recreation activities to enhance revenue generation. Given the exceptionally vast resources of the area, these purposes are appropriate if they are properly planned and supervised.

The Lower Zambezi National Park is significant because of its close proximity to the capital Lusaka, its wide variety of recreation activities, its spectacular scenery and abundant wildlife species, and its location on the imposing Zambezi River, just opposite another protected area, Mana Pools. It forms part of a 16,800 km² contiguous wildlife area, the largest continuous protected area in the region.

The management objectives for Lower Zambezi National Park have been established in the following categories:

- *Natural resources:* to ensure that the bio-diversity and abundance of indigenous fauna and flora and habitats are maintained while protecting the endangered and threatened species;
- *Cultural resources in the park and surrounding game management areas (GMAs):* to ensure the protection and integrity of all cultural heritage of the area in accordance with local tradition;
- *Visitor use:* to ensure that tourist visitor requirements are met while maintaining the natural resource management objectives;
- *Tourism development:* to provide a high quality, low-impact tourist infrastructure for a low volume of high-market ecotourists, while maintaining the pristine nature of the park;
- *Local community:* to focus on the active participation and involvement of communities in the surrounding GMAs in sustaining the resources, while sharing the benefits and minimizing any resource use conflicts between wildlife managers and the local communities.

RESEARCH METHODOLOGY

The research methodology was designed to focus on three aspects: the appraisal of existing tourist resources and activities in the area; identification of significant impacts; and development of mitigation measures for the identified significant impacts.

Data collection was competed through three separate tasks.

Task one

The first task was to identify the existing tourist resources and activities in the Lower Zambezi National Park. This task involved fieldwork to collect data on the physical environment of the area, such as climate, topography, geology, soils, hydrology, water resources, air quality, fauna and flora.

This data collection started with an extensive secondary data search, mainly from the research unit library of the Department of National Parks and Wildlife Services at Chilanga. Data on the fauna was obtained from aerial and ground counts of wildlife compiled by the NPWS. Through the completion of a literature search, a list was compiled of mammals, birds, reptiles, amphibians and fish in the area. These were verified by actual sightings during the fieldwork by animal sighting records kept at some of the lodges.

The main vegetation types were ascertained using a vegetation map, topographic map and aerial photographs. Representative vegetation shades and tones were identified on the aerial photographs using table stereoscopes. Ground truthing was then done in the field to determine the key tree species in the representative areas by use of line transects.

Water samples were collected from a number of points suspected to be affected by effluent and sewage seepage from the tourist camps along the Zambezi. The samples were tested for faecal chloroforms at the environmental engineering laboratory at the University of Zambia to determine the level of contamination of the water due to human activity.

To establish the existing tourist activities, the area was visited for a couple of weeks during the fieldwork. The information was gathered using structured questionnaires to interview the tour operators and wildlife scouts working in the area. This was complemented by a review of literature from tourist marketing brochures for the Lower Zambezi National Park obtained from the tour operators and the Zambia National Tourist Board (ZNTB) in Lusaka.

Task two

The objective of this part of the study was to identify the significant environmental and socio-economic impacts of tourism development in the Lower Zambezi National Park and the surrounding game management areas. An assessment was made of potential and actual individual and cumulative impacts of tourist activities on the natural resource base and socio-economic conditions. The first step was a preliminary impact identification and prediction for all major tourist investments in the area.

A systematic impact identification matrix was used. This was based on the assertion that interactions between the environment and tourism development inputs, activities and outputs lead to environmental and socio-economic impacts.

The impact identification matrix was designed to exhaustively assess the likely impacts on the physical and human environment (Wathern, 1988).

Impacts were identified on air, soil, water, vegetation, wildlife, cultural heritage and the local communities in the surrounding GMAs. The likely impacts identified were then investigated physically during fieldwork, to assess their presence, magnitude and significance as evaluated against the Lower Zambezi National Park purpose, significance and management objectives. In addition to this, extensive consultations were made with National Parks and Wildlife Services, Zambia National Tourist Board, tour operators, the Tourism Council of Zambia, the Wildlife and Environmental Conservation Society of Zambia, the World Wildlife Fund and the International Union for the Conservation of Nature (IUCN) on their major environmental concerns for the area.

The assessment was done separately for the impacts on the five physical environment parameters and the two human environment parameters. Identification of individual impacts of different tourist activities and associated inputs and outputs were assessed as broadly as possible to cover all potential effects on the natural environment. Impact assessment encompassed positive and negative, cumulative, short-term and long-term, permanent and temporal, direct and indirect, and reversible and irreversible impacts. This was completed using three broad categories.

The first category assessed the impacts of light charter planes, vehicles on the main access road, vehicles on loop roads, power boats and canoes on the Zambezi. These were assessed for their likely impacts on vegetation destruction, soil erosion, soil compaction, wildlife disturbance, habitat destruction, littering, water and air pollution, noise, fire risks and weed introduction along roads and riverbanks.

The second category assessed the environmental impacts of tourist campsites within the national park. These were assessed in terms of likely impacts from construction work, the use period and the off-season period (abandoned structures). The likely environmental impacts considered included vegetation destruction, soil erosion, soil compaction, riverbank erosion, wildlife disturbance or habitat destruction, firewood collection (Huxtable, 1987), littering, sewage disposal, water pollution, noise, visual impressions, and overexploitation of local resources such as water, labour and construction materials.

The third category assessed the impacts of the various recreation activities on the natural environment. The activities assessed included game drives, walking safaris, canoeing safaris, boat cruise activities, bird watching, bush walks and sport fishing. The environmental receptors considered for each activity were air, water, soil, vegetation, wildlife and cultural heritage.

The indicators of cumulative effects used on the physical environment were ecological indicators such as vegetation damage, localized deforestation, water quality, soil erosion as indicated by the presence of off-road tracks, and wildlife species as indicated by species diversity, and the presence or absence of endangered species. In addition, the changing behaviour of wildlife in the presence of humans was used as an indicator of the impacts of the tourist activities on wildlife. On the positive side, the potential effects of having people in the area acting as a deterrent to poaching in the national park was also considered.

To identify and assess socio-economic impacts related to tourism development, data was collected on the economic, social and cultural dimensions of the local population in the surrounding game management area. The issues assessed were the demands and pressures on local resources such as water, forests, wildlife, fisheries, and access to land and other productive resources. Lastly, information was collected on the local community's economic benefits and costs related to tourism development. The information gathered included employment creation for local people, increased market opportunities for the local population, and increased household incomes in the community.

After potential impacts were identified, the study further identified the major significant impacts. This was done by taking into consideration the following factors: types of impacts, magnitude and importance of the impacts identified, intensity of impacts, extent of impacts in terms of area affected, sensitivity and uniqueness of affected environments and infringement upon environmental laws. At the end of this exercise, a comprehensive list of all significant impacts identified was compiled.

Task three

The final task of the study was to develop a mitigation plan for environmental and socio-economic impacts of tourism development in the Lower Zambezi National Park and the surrounding game management area. After identifying the significant environmental and socio-economic impacts, a thorough assessment of alternative mitigation measures to ameliorate impacts commenced. There was an assessment of alternative designs of transportation infrastructure, accommodation structures, and operational and organizational arrangements of tourist activities likely to cause environmental degradation.

These mitigation measures took into account technical, ecological, economic and social dimensions. Suggested mitigation alternatives considered suitability of local conditions, institutional capacities and environmental monitoring requirements relative to the available resources. The final result of this task was a set of mitigation measures for reducing or eliminating the increased environmental impacts of tourism developments in the Lower Zambezi National Park.

RESEARCH FINDINGS

The results of the research are presented in three sections:
- the details of the tourist resources and activities in the area;
- the significant impacts identified as a result of these activities;
- and the mitigation measures suggested for minimizing the identified impacts.

Tourist resources and activities in the Lower Zambezi National Park

This area's greatest asset is the variety and diversity of natural resources within a small geographical distance. The diversity of habitats in the Lower Zambezi National Park and surrounding GMAs is the single most important resource of the area. The area has a variety of landforms, which include the river system, the valley floor, escarpment, hills and the plateau. Correspondingly, the area contains a wide range of ecosystems and habitats. These include woodlands, grasslands, islands, flood plains, rivers, lagoons, mountains, salt pans and springs. This mosaic of habitats supports a great diversity of wildlife within a small area.

The Lower Zambezi area is home to a wide variety of mammals, reptiles, birds, amphibians, fish and insects. The park has both small and large mammals in abundance. The large mammals occupy the miombo woodlands of the plateau and escarpment, woodland fringes, riverine forests, the plains, flood plains, lagoons, dambos and the Zambezi River. A major ecological feature of wildlife in LZNP is the seasonal movement of large mammals in response to the availability of food and water (Yonenda and Mwima, 1995). The riparian woodlands on the Zambezi alluvial terraces are a dry-season concentration zone for many species because plant productivity is more abundant on these terraces in the late dry season than on the rest of the valley floor and the bordering escarpment. The *acacia albida,* the dominant tree species of the alluvial system, is of particular importance for browsing and for shade, as it has an enormous foliage cycle. It is leafless in the wet season but leafs and bears protein-rich pods in the dry season. As a result, seasonal changes in the distribution of large mammals have been observed. The animals are widely dispersed in the wet season when there is plenty of water and green pasture throughout the area. In the dry season, the animals are largely concentrated along the valley and islands on the river because most of the areas inland have no water and the grass is dry (see Figure 7.2).

Figure 7.2 Animal distribution in the dry season – Lower Zambezi National Park

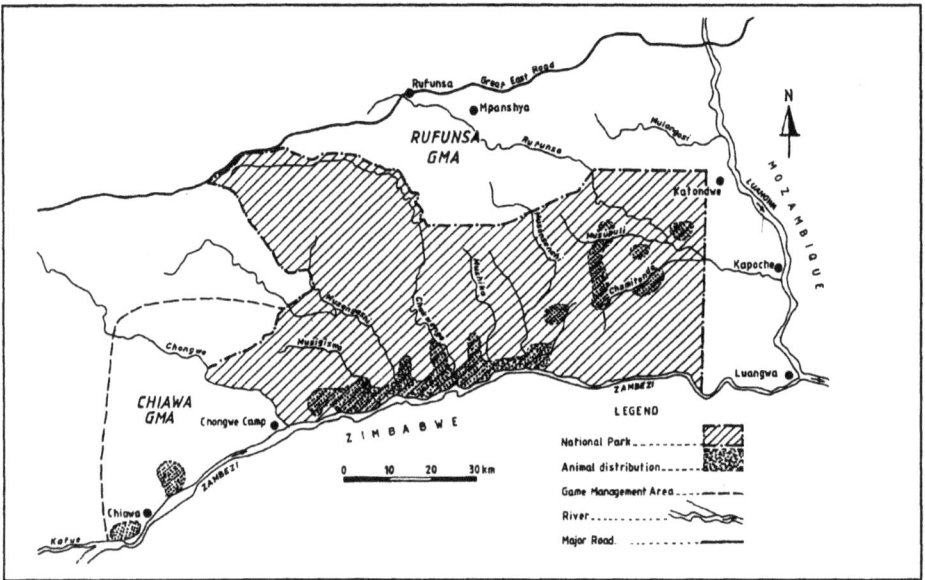

The Zambezi River has a large concentration of reptiles including Nile crocodiles of all sizes. Crocodiles are also found in the major tributaries of the Zambezi and in lagoons.

The national park's varied habitats support a wide variety and abundance of bird life, with more than 300 species recorded. The birds are evenly distributed, though the highest concentrations are along the Zambezi River and other wetlands. Ornithological studies are required to ascertain the common habitats of each key species.

The Zambezi River, its tributaries and lagoons boast a variety of fish species, some of which are important for both commercial and sport fishing. It is important that scientific studies be made of the fish types in the Lower Zambezi segment of the Zambezi River system, as this section of the river is an ecological island delimited by the Kariba dam upstream and Cabbora Basa dams downstream. These two artificial barriers prevent fish movement from upstream and downstream, which was not the case before these dams were erected. This artificial separation has produced negative effects on the fish in the Lower Zambezi segment.

Most of the life forms of the area are associated with the Zambezi River and its offshoots. These include the Kafue, Chongwe, Chakwenga, Musensenshi, and the Luangwa rivers. These rivers provide water and riverine vegetation for the wildlife in the area. The lands along these tributaries are relatively wet for most of the year and provide green pastures and forage for Hill Miombo wildlife such as sable, eland and roan antelope.

There are several islands along the Zambezi River. Some of these emerged recently, following the impoundment of water at Kariba dam and the droughts experienced in this region during the 1980s. Though most of these islands are relatively unstable, they provide added habitat. Most of them are colonized by *acacia* tree species and grasses which provide green pastures and forage for large mammals such as hippo, elephant and buffalo, especially in the dry season when most of the grass elsewhere is dry. The Zambezi River meanders through the valley as it is guided by the physiography of the area. Over time, the river has changed course in a number of places and has created several oxbow lakes. These have become important habitats for aquatic wildlife such as hippo, crocodile and fish.

The mountain range and escarpment on the northern boundary of the area is aligned in a generally northeast-southwest direction. The escarpment that rises to about 1200m (a.s.l) is deeply dissected by massive ridges of various heights towering over the valley floor. The rugged ridges are dissected by numerous drainage lines which provide spectacular scenery.

The Lower Zambezi area is rich in cultural heritage. Several historic and archaeological sites are located there: the Kanyemba Island where Dr. David Livingstone rested during his trans-African journeys; the site of Senior Chief Mburuma's old village, before the area was declared a national park; and Old Feira, where the Portuguese first settled – one of the oldest modern-day settlements in this part of the country.

Tourist facilities in the Lower Zambezi National Park

The park's facilities include tourist accommodation, camp sites, hides, loop roads and other amenities. The immense potential of the national park has given rise to tourist activities that attract scores of local, regional and international visitors to the Lower Zambezi. In response to the influx of tourists, more accommodation facilities have been developed. These include lodges and campsites.

There are a total of nine tourist camps operating in the park for seven months in a year, from May to November. These camps provide a total of 11,288 room nights and 24,610 bed nights for the duration of the tourist season. All of them are located along the park's 120-kilometer river frontage, spaced at average intervals of about 10 kilometres. However, most of them are located in a 65-kilometre length of river frontage where game viewing is claimed to be most viable (see Figure 7.3).

Figure 7.3 Tourist camps and access roads in the Lower Zambezi National Park

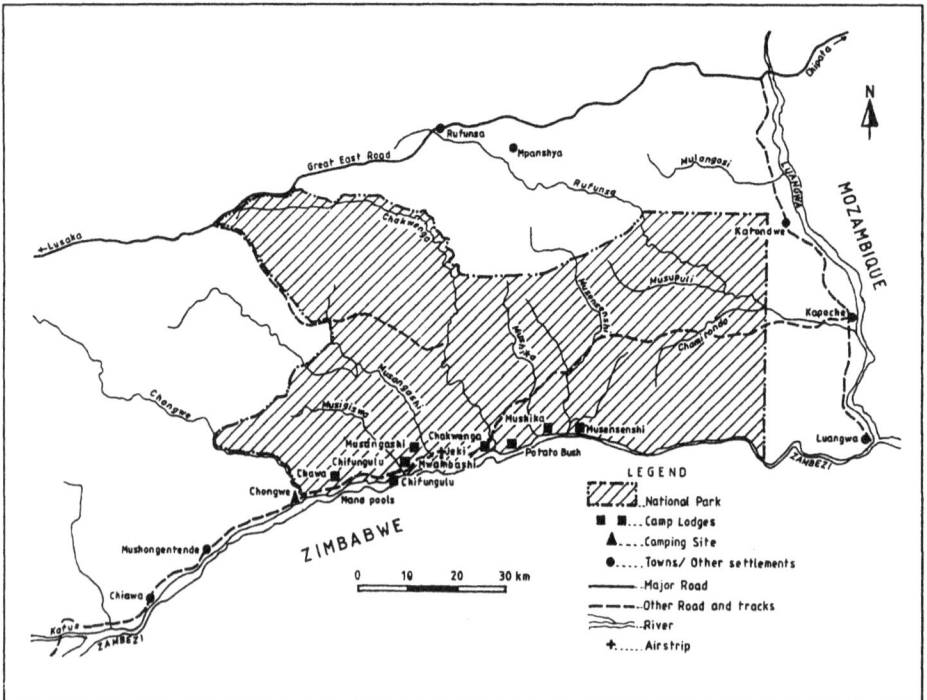

All the camps have assumed different architectural characteristics in design and elevation. The only common characteristic is the treatment of the roofs and supporting frames, which are mainly of thatch and poles. A number of camps, however, are tented and have canvas walls and roofs.

In recent years, there has been an increase in both visitor numbers and motorized transport entering the national park. Park statistics indicate that 4,159 tourists entered the park between January and October 1997. This is an average of 416 people visiting the park each month, or 14 people per day.

During the same period in 1997, a total of 520 vehicles entered the park, an increase of more than 300% over the previous year. Similarly, airstrip landings increased from 8 in 1995 to 106 by October of 1997. These vehicle numbers do not include the resident vehicles kept at each camp for viewing game and delivering supplies. On average, each tourist camp has two vehicles for game viewing and one for logistical support. This means there are an additional 30 vehicles in the park at a time.

Table 7.1 Number of visitors and motorized traffic to the Lower Zambezi National Park

YEAR	VISITORS	VEHICLES	LANDINGS
1995	2480	146	08
1996	2540	150	50
1997*	4159	520	106

*The 1997 figures are up to October only.

There is no doubt that the numbers of visitors, vehicles, boats and aircraft landings in the Lower Zambezi National Park have increased. This has attracted investment to the area and underscores the need to consider the consequences for the environment and the tourist industry's sustainablility.

Tourist activities

The main tourist activities in Lower Zambezi are game viewing, boating, canoeing, sport fishing, bird watching, safari walking, and research work. In Zambia, game viewing is done in open vans mounted with seats. Day game drives take place in the early morning or late afternoon. Night drives are normally done from around 1800 hours to about 2100 hours. The drives are along narrow, winding loop roads.

Boating is often combined with other tourist activities such as fishing, bird watching, etc. In the Lower Zambezi, speedboats of up to 90 horsepower are used to carry as many as six passengers. Canoeing parties launch their canoes accompanied by a paddler/guide and travel downstream for a few days. Canoeing offers opportunities for seeing game and birds, as a lot of animals are attracted to the river banks, especially in the dry season. Tourists who enjoy fishing, angle for species such as the tiger fish and vundu. Sometimes the fish caught are returned to the water to avoid adversely affecting the fish populations.

Bird watching is a specialized tourist activity, which includes both scientific study (ornithology) and the mere enjoyment of observing bird life in a natural and undisturbed environment. Walking safaris are conducted to enable the tourist to see and photograph game at close range.

Finally, research is also done at the park, which often involves the study of certain unique ecosystems or rare fauna and flora.

Tourism Development Impacts in the Lower Zambezi National Park

Sources of impacts

In addition to the recreational activities which cause damage, the construction of infrastructure to support tourism is also of concern. There are significant environmental impacts during the construction of camps and accommodations. Preparation and installation of support infrastructure, transportation and energy use damage the environment. The tourism outputs which have negative impacts are excessive use of construction materials, domestic waste, sewage sludge, off-road tracks, ecological changes, landscape changes and bad visual impressions.

Impacts on the Zambezi River and river frontage

The location of many of the camps along the river frontage constitutes a major threat to the river ecology and its relatively pristine vegetation. Inadequately designed sewage disposal systems for shower rooms and flush toilets were positioned within three metres of the river, so untreated sewage is polluting the river. In addition, the disposal of solid waste in shallow pits has resulted in littering around the tourist camps and attracted scavenging hyenas.

There has been some indiscriminate clearing of vegetation on camp sites along the banks of the river. This habitat destruction may be contributing to species loss. In addition, the location and design of riverbank camp sites have marred the views from the river and other vantage points in the park. This is slowly spoiling the wilderness and solitary experience for which the park is famous.

Recreational boating has caused a number of problems. In the dry season, when tourist activity is highest, power boats damage fish eggs in substrates of sand and mud in the shallow river waters. The boats generate excessive waves which have caused extensive riverbank erosion. Boat launching bays or jetties are not constructed to any acceptable standard, causing serious bank erosion at the tourist campsites. The loop roads constructed close to the riverbanks contribute to further erosion.

Although river water samples did not show serious organic contamination, the leakage and spillage of petroleum products from power boats may sooner or later lead to water pollution. This is particularly likely to occur given that the controlling authority does not inspect boats used on the river.

Impacts on vegetation

The major threat to the vegetation in the area is off-road drives by game viewing parties and the indiscriminate clearing of campsites. A number of off-road drives by game viewing vehicles were observed during fieldwork. Trampling of vegetation by car tires over time has damaged plant shoots. At tourist development sites, the introduction of exotic plant species such as carpet grasses and banana trees is a threat to the indigenous plant ecology, the park's natural vegetation.

Impacts on wildlife

A major threat to large mammals in the park is the introduction of exotic animal species such as cats, which were found at some of the tourist camps. However, the actual impact of this situation is still difficult to quantify.

Noise disturbance from vehicles, aircraft and boats was observed to be one of the most evident impacts of tourism development in the area. There is uncontrolled, congested boat and vehicle traffic in a small area currently used for game viewing. The noise disturbs the animals and interrupts their daily activities of hunting, feeding and mating. Tourist camps have been built by the river channels along the animals' migration routes, restricting their free movement from the escarpment to the river for water and greener pasture in the dry season.

There does not appear to be any serious immediate threat to the bird life in the area. However, with poor sewage and solid waste disposal along the river, contaminated water may seriously threaten aquatic bird life.

Sport fishing for tiger fish, if increased further, may have adverse effects on the stock. The indications are that the catch per effort has declined over the past years. There have been a few incidences of fish injured due to the use of wrong fishing gear.

The use of firewood inside the park is a major threat to dry wood insect species such as wood beetles, which die when ground wood is burned in camp fires at night (Ringewaldt, 1984).

Impacts on soils

Soil erosion is one of the major impacts of tourism identified in the park. Soil erosion is exacerbated by activities like off-road driving by irresponsible and poorly trained tour guides. Off road driving, especially in wet areas, has created ditches which have eventually worsened to become incipient gullies. Soil erosion is accelerated by poorly routed loop roads built without adequate supervision and control. Tour operators construct the loop roads to their convenience and when the roads are too close to the river, the bank collapses. The poor drainage system around the badly situated airstrip has led to increased surface runoff.

Impacts on cultural heritage sites

The major threat to cultural heritage sites are human activities and tourist facilities on the sites or nearby. Planners did not consult local communities in selecting sites for tourist infrastructure development. There is a lack of proper documentation of the area's cultural heritage to help inform site selection decisions.

Socio-economic impacts

Employment has been created for the local communities and has increased household incomes. However, those employed in the tourist establishments receive low wages averaging about US$30 per month. The local people are hired, often as unskilled labour.

MITIGATION MEASURES FOR SIGNIFICANT IMPACTS

What can be done to change these negative impacts so that tourism benefits can be maximized for all concerned and for the environment? The mitigation measures proposed here are potential remedial actions for each of the significant negative impacts identified by the research.

Mitigation of impacts on the Zambezi River and river frontage

There is need to put in place strict controls for all tourist infrastructure and facility developments. These should include establishing a safe distance from the Zambezi River frontage for all infrastructure. The infrastructure standards set by the Zambia National Tourist Board must be enforced by the NPWS.

The design of the waste disposal systems in the tourist camps should be approved by the Environmental Council of Zambia. These standards should be re-examined in view of the current environmental hazards posed by the existing waste disposal systems along the river.

There must also be close regulation and monitoring of all tourist activities to reduce congestion caused by too many boats and canoes in the park at any given time. The NPWS must devise a system for controlling water traffic on each river segment.

The hull size of boats should be limited. The use of marine-grade aluminum boats would be preferable, to help reduce the drag and wash which affect the shoreline. In sensitive shore zones, the boat speeds must be limited to levels that will not cause harm. Boats should not be allowed to have more than 40 horsepower. Boat driving techniques can have a considerable bearing on the river environment. Reckless driving, applying full throttle to a jet unit directed towards a sand bank or operating a propeller in shallow, muddy water will obviously cause considerable disturbance. All such dangerous boating should be prohibited. Finally, all launch sites and jetties must be constructed to meet international standards in order to prevent riverbank erosion.

The game viewing loop roads should be constructed away from the river to avoid the congestion of game viewing vehicles in the dry season, when animals congregate there for water and greener pasture. More game viewing loop roads should be constructed towards the escarpment to disperse the traffic during the peak tourist season. These should be all-weather roads to handle tourist activity throughout the year to help reduce congestion in the dry season.

Mitigation of impacts on mammals

Vehicles on game viewing drives should obey the stipulated speed limit of 40 kilometres per hour in the park to minimize dust, noise, and accidental killing of the wildlife. There should be more tourist loop roads in the park to improve the vehicle-to-open-road-ratio and reduce the impacts of noise and wildlife disturbance. Tourist activities should be regulated by the NPWS to lessen congestion and overcrowding around key wildlife species to avoid disturbance during the animals' essential biological activities such as feeding and mating. Environment awareness education is needed for tour guides and tourists to avoid detrimental behaviour or activities, such as off-road drives. Tour guides must be trained and qualified. The NPWS can handle the certification of tour guides, as it is the controlling body for national parks.

Mitigation of impacts on fish, insects, vegetation and soils

Tour operators in the area should minimize the impact on selected fish species (e.g. tiger fish) by adopting a catch and release policy for sports fishing. This policy should be supported by educational awareness campaigns for anglers, with booklets and leaflets provided at all tourist camps. In addition, either fisheries or wildlife officers should monitor sport-fishing activities. It is also suggested that only fishing gear approved by the fisheries department and the Tourism Council of Zambia should be used for sport fishing to reduce injuries to fish.

Fuel wood collection within the park should be prohibited to minimize the loss of dry wood species which are insect habitats.

The plots leased for tourism developments in the park should be reduced from 5 hectares to 2.5 hectares to minimize unnecessary clearing of vegetation. The research conducted in this study indicates that about half of the allocated plots have been used for tourist camps and, in many cases, vegetation clearing went well beyond the developed areas. The control measures suggested for mammal protection, such as minimizing off-road drives, would also have a positive effect on reducing vegetation damage.

The loop roads and other tourist infrastructure should be professionally surveyed in order to prevent soil erosion and runoff in the rainy season.

Mitigation of impacts on cultural heritage

Tourism has an impact on cultural heritage primarily because lodges and other forms of tourist infrastructure have been placed on or very near cultural heritage sites. The location of activities, buildings and roadways to be developed should be decided upon in consultation with the local communities and the National Heritage Conservation Commission. There should be a comprehensive inventory of all the cultural heritage sites in the area. These measures will facilitate cultural sensitivity as ecotourism is developed in the area.

Mitigation of socio-economic impacts

To reinforce tourism's positive impacts on the community, it is suggested that more local people be recruited at the senior managerial level.

CONCLUSIONS

With improved planning and management, the Lower Zambezi National Park should be able to attract more and more international tourists to Zambia, without placing undue stress on the environment or the people living in the area. This study has demonstrated, however, that present tourism development in the park is beginning to have serious environmental consequences. The following recommendations are offered to correct these problems:

▪ It is essential to develop a park management plan which is highly participatory, engages all stakeholders and strikes a balance between resource conservation and tourism development. The management plan should include guidelines for tourist campsite location, acceptable tourist facility standards, and general EIA guidelines for tourist site development and facilities. The plan should have legal backing and mechanisms should be put in place to enforce it. In addition, there should be codes of conduct for tour operators, host communities, and tourists. The management plan should also zone the park into areas for various uses which should not conflict with each other or harm the environment. Regulation and control of the tourist numbers, vehicles, and activities should be specified. The plan should be accompanied by skill development for National Parks and Wildlife Service personnel.

▪ A surveillance system to ensure compliance with effective regulations requires capable wildlife scouts. Non-complying operators should be fined, and those who comply with the tourism environmental codes of conduct should be rewarded.

▶ An environmental awareness campaign needs to be established. Visitors need to be informed about the purpose and significance of the Lower Zambezi National Park. An interpretative program for visitors should also be established so that visitors understand the fragility of the area's resources.

▶ A monitoring and evaluation program needs to be established so that management can ensure that the ecology and environment are not degraded. Management must be able to observe and evaluate any changes to the surroundings that may be caused by tourism development. This requires an adaptive management strategy which allows for timely identification of significant changes to ensure appropriate counter strategies. This can be done effectively through monitoring the park's major animal and plant species to provide information on their condition and distribution over time. The information may serve as a basis for sound conservation and management policies and decisions. Soil erosion should be monitored by establishing benchmarks to indicate current soil levels in areas where there is significant erosion. Any change in the graduated level from previous levels will indicate the magnitude of soil loss. This information can be used for the routing of the park's roadways.

▶ Cultural resource management is also a key factor in environmental sustainability. It is recommended that a detailed inventory be made of all cultural, historic and archaeological sites in the park and surrounding GMAs. This will help ensure the protection of all the cultural heritage resources according to the traditional requirements of the local people.

REFERENCES

Buckley, R. and Pannell, J. 1990: Environmental impacts of tourism and recreation in national parks and conservation reserves. *The Journal of Tourism Studies,* 1 (1), 24-32.

Dalal-Clayton, D.B. 1985: The development of soil survey in Zambia. *Soil Survey and Land Evaluation,* 4, 18-23.

DCEC. 1993: *Environmental Manual, Environmental Procedures and Methodology Governing Lome IV Development Co-operation Projects.* Development Commission of the European Communities.

Edmonds, A.C.R. 1976: *The Vegetation Map of Zambia.* Map Sheet No. 7. Lusaka: GRZ, Forest Department.

EPPCA. 1990: *The Environmental Protection and Pollution Control Act, No.12,* 1990. Lusaka: ECZ-MENR.

Handlos, W.L. and Haward, G.W. 1985: *Development Prospects for the Zambezi Valley in Zambia.* Lusaka: University of Zambia, Kafue Basin Research Committee.

Huxtable, D. 1987: *The Environmental Impact of Firewood Collection for Campfires and Appropriate Management Strategies.* Salisbury: South Australian College of Advanced Education.

Matheison, A. and Wall, G. 1982: *Tourism: Economic, Physical and Social Impact.* London: Longmans.

Muliya, M. 1997: *EIA Procedures and Requirements in Zambia.* Lusaka: ECZ.

NPWS. 1992: *Outline Management Plan for Lower Zambezi National Park.* Chilanga: NPWS, Ministry of Tourism.

Ringewaldt, D. 1984: Firewood usage in parks. *Australian Ranger Bulletin,* 3 (1), 11.

Sichingabula, H.M. 1997: *Physical Characteristics of the Lower Zambezi National Park and Adjacent Game Management Areas.* Chilanga: EDF-NPWS.

University of Zambia. 1987: *The Resources of the Middle Zambezi Valley.* Lusaka: University of Zambia, River Basin Research Committee.

Wathern, P. (ed.). 1988: *Environmental Impact Assessment: Theory and Practice.* London: Unwin Hyman.

World Bank. 1991: *Environmental Assessment Sourcebook.* Volume II Sectoral Guidelines. Washington D.C.: World Bank.

Yonenda, K. and Mwima, H.M. 1995: *Report on the Aerial Census of Large Mammals in Lower Zambezi National Park.* Chilanga: NPWS.

Chapter 8

THE APPLICATION OF TRADITIONAL FOLK METHODS OF COMMUNICATION TO ECOTOURISM DEVELOPMENT IN TSWAING, SOUTH AFRICA

by Valerie Baron

INTRODUCTION

Traditional theories and approaches to development have largely ignored or bypassed the importance and utility of local culture and knowledge in decision-making. However, the current impasse in development thinking may allow for newer, unconventional and culturally sensitive approaches to gain acceptance. The 1980s have seen what is referred to as a "paradigm shift", "another development" or "alternative development". This shift is usually described as a movement away from the concept of development communication (DC) with its emphasis on top-down, big-media-centered, government-to-people communication, to development support communication (DSC) focused on co-equal, little-media-centered, government-with-people communication (Ascroft and Masilela, 1989). The DSC approach should not simply be based on a "co-equal knowledge sharing", but should also explore the potential of culture in facilitating development. This is particularly relevant for ecotourism development. An excellent example of culture incorporated into ecotourism strategies is the use of folk media, or, as it will be referred to in this chapter, traditional folk methods of communication (TFMC). In this research, folk methods of communication are applied in the Tswaing crater in South Africa to promote environmental education for visitors to a local crater, the centre of attraction.

TFMCs are communication methods used by many people, particularly in rural areas, and include (but are not restricted to) poetry, songs and other oral traditions that have been passed down from generation to generation. The most suitable definition for this study includes elements of verbal, mural and visual forms familiar to, and appreciated by, the rural people (Feliciano, in UNESCO, 1982). The central functions of these communication methods are to entertain, inform, instruct, publicize, raise consciousness and enlighten through dialogue and in a sometimes interactive manner (Kidd, 1982; Madu, 1986).

TFMCs have the potential to contribute to grassroots development because they represent a departure from conventional development ideas. Traditionally, international development projects and theories have concentrated on imposing new ideas and models on local populations. The existing culture was generally viewed as an obstacle to development. Kidd and Colletta (1980), however, suggest that one reason this has occurred is because culture has perhaps been too difficult or too abstract to appraise or incorporate into decision-making strategies. According to Kidd and Colletta (1980, p. 13):

> ...existing cultural structures can be identified and used to carry development messages and mobilized to encourage mass participation in the development process through the sensitive modification and adaptation of their multiple function. In this matter, culture can be used as a foundation for, rather than as a barrier, to change.

Many communication experts who have adopted the approach of using culture in development strategies have incorporated folk forms into their work. However, there is still much work to be done in this field. The aim of this research is to attempt to help fill that gap in the South African context.

In South Africa, between 1950 and 1955, the Parliament passed several apartheid acts (De Jong; personal communication, 1997). One of these, the Population Registration Act, imposed a policy that classified people according to skin color, descent and language (De Jong, 1997). Those whom the Population Registration Act classified as requiring relocation were forced to resettle in the Tswaing area. The cultures represented in the area today include: Zulu, Xhoxa, northern and southern Sotho, Tsonga, Ndebele, Venda, Nogni and other groups. Also, in recent years many people have migrated to the area from Mozambique, Zimbabwe and Botswana in search of employment. Because of this migration, the population of the Tswaing region has increased to more than two million people (De Jong and Reimold, 1995).

Due to the massive population increase, jobs have become scarce leaving many people in secondary and informal jobs. This rather dense population has put a strain on the local environment. Waste pollution and water contamination have led to sanitary and health problems. The environmental problems in the informal and unplanned settlement areas stem from a lack of appropriate decision-making and commitment to the environment.

As the study area is overpopulated and the unplanned settlements pose a threat to the environment, addressing these issues in the region is essential. The study reported here focuses on people's knowledge of environmental issues as reflected in their cultural practices, and how knowledge and cultural practices could prove useful in building environmental awareness. This research investigated the existing local cultural communication channels or TFMCs and attempted to determine how they may be useful in fostering environmental awareness and promoting environmental education in Tswaing. The intent of the study was not to impose new ideas upon the inhabitants, but to present ideas in a way that was familiar and recognizable to local people. To reach this goal, several objectives were formulated. They are as follows:

1. To become acquainted with cultural practices and processes of the area, particularly existing cultural forms of communication;
2. To identify different TFMCs and study their potential contributions to environmental education;
3. To effectively work with some artists in a team atmosphere to produce TFMCs for environmental awareness; and
4. To study TFMCs in order to establish whether they can be applied effectively to foster environmental awareness.

The premise of this research: if ideas are presented in recognizable terms, such as the local idiom, riddles and proverbs which are predominant folk forms in Africa (Jones, 1995), rural populations are more likely to accept and value them. The nature of the problem is that if information is imposed and not interwoven with existing cultural communication channels, messages may not be understood or accepted. Making new information compatible with the existing system will likely increase the effectiveness of communication. Therefore, integrating cultural communication channels for ecotourism purposes could be a powerful instrument for facilitating environmental awareness in others.

Study Area

Tswaing Crater Museum in South Africa was established in 1993 under the auspices of the National Cultural History Museum (NCHM). Tswaing (pronounced tswa-ing), which means "place of salt" in Tswana, is situated about 40 km northwest of Pretoria within the Gauteng province.

Tswaing crater was formed about 220,000 years ago when a meteorite crashed into the earth's crust of the Zoutpan area (now Tswaing). This natural formation is one of the youngest and best preserved meteorite impact sites in the world (Hatting and Moolman, 1996). It has generated salt and soda ash from earlier times which has attracted people for thousands of years.

About 100,000 years ago, salt generated from the crater allowed local inhabitants and farmers, mainly the Tswana, Sotho, and Ndebele, to trade salt with other groups for cattle, weapons, ornaments and iron (De Jong, 1996: De Jong and Reimold, 1995). They also used the mineral for flavouring their food and for preserving leather and meat.

By 1836 white farmers settled in the area and started mining the crater for salt and soda ash (De Jong, 1996). The crater became the property of the Zuid-Africkkanshe Republiek in 1858 and strict control of mining was implemented (De Jong, 1996). As Tswaing was South Africa's only source of soda and salt, a commercial company called South African Alkaly Ltd was established around the turn of the century to mine the area (Damaneyt, 1995; De Jong, 1996). From 1912 to 1956, soda and some salt were mined, processed and exported (Kussel, 1996b). Donkey wagons transported the extracted soda ash to Hammanskraal (Kussel, 1996a). Consequently, by the mid-1950s the soda reserves were exploited to such an extent that the state decided to close the factory (Kussel, 1996b). The Zoutpan farm (Tswaing), upon which the crater was situated, became known as one of the most overgrazed farms in Gauteng, as a result of the damage done by the donkeys and mules used for transportation (Kussel, 1996b).

After the factory closed in 1956, the state decided to have the Department of Agriculture initiate an agricultural research station to re-establish the lost vegetation. They ran the area as an experimental cattle-breeding farm and established an effective rotation system based on a subdivision of the farm according to its eight soil types and eight ecosystems (Hatting and Moolman, 1996). This system of rotation was so successful that the once nearly ruined farm is known today as one of the best examples of mixed bushveld farming (Kussel,

1996b). The farm also became a research laboratory for agriculturalists, geologists, entomologists and anthropologists.

In the mid-1980s, another threat to the area emerged. New people moved into the area surrounding Tswaing, settling in Winterveld, Kromkuil, Nuwe Eersterus and Sosanguve. It is estimated that the area became one of the most densely populated areas on the African continent (De Jong and Reimold, 1995). As the new settlers needed them, firewood, building materials, food, fences, trees and cattle began to disappear from the Zoutpan farm. The problem became so severe that the Department of Agriculture considered abandoning the farm and crater (Kussel, 1996b).

An environmental museum

With the impending change in government and priorities anticipated with the 1994 election, the National Cultural History Museum (NCHM) became aware of the imminent closure of the research station and initiated negotiations with the state to take over the Zoutpan farm. The NCHM believed that the site was of international importance due to the crater and surrounding ecosystems and wanted to develop it into an open-air environmental museum (Coller, Damaneyt, De Jong, Kussel and Reimold, 1995).

The museum took over the farm on January 1, 1993 with the aim of involving the surrounding communities in its development (Kussel, 1996b). The NCHM initiated a needs assessment and identified needs for:

a)   cultural conservation
b)   wildlife/nature conservation
c)   recreation
d)   education, training and research
e)   tourism, and
f)   regional community development.

Additionally, the emphasis was on planning "with" instead of planning "for" people (Kussel, 1996a). The rationale that people would not take responsibility or ownership for the project unless they were intimately involved was established in the planning process. Through a long and, in many cases, arduous process of consultation and joint decision-making, the museum developed a master plan that was acceptable to all involved (Damaneyt, 1995). The communities took responsibility for the protection of the farm and its resources. As a result, theft of fences and animals was reduced to a minimum. An educational walking trail was developed, and a programme which emphasizes cutting invasive trees for income generation is now running successfully. A recycling project was started, which encourages local school children to pay for their visit by bringing empty cans. The number of school groups and tourists visiting the crater is increasing and, consequently, the NCHM is planning to develop both an arts and crafts centre and an environmental education facility.

By involving the local people in this project, the NCHM achieved what many people thought impossible. Though many challenges still lie ahead, the Tswaing project has thus far succeeded in conserving and developing a unique site as a tourist attraction as well as a resource for raw materials.

Methodology

For this study, establishing a qualitative research methodology was necessary. Ethnographic, exploratory and descriptive approaches were the main methods used. The research was based on participant observation and employed on site focus groups and personal interviews to identify the cultural context and to interview folk artists who have the potential to provide environmental education. The four objectives of the study are listed below with respect to appropriate research techniques.

The first objective was to become acquainted with the cultural practices and processes of the area, particularly existing cultural forms of communication. Initiating a number of participatory exercises, such as participatory mappings and the use of an interactive journal to identify key informants and key artists for the study, addressed this objective. Those who identified cultural and environmental features were interviewed for further clarification. The methods employed in the study were designed to be culturally sensitive, with hopes of establishing a rapport with the local people.

The second objective was to identify different TFMCs and study their potential contributions to environmental education. The objective was to generate a "book of basic data", as suggested by Ranganath (1980a, 1980b), in the form of an inventory of the folk forms under study. Observations and semi-structured interviews were conducted for this purpose. All information was recorded and interpreted to identify artists who were or could contribute to environmental education. The "book of basic data" (ibid.) also provided concrete information on whether a particular folk form was appropriate or inappropriate for conveying certain environmental messages.

The third objective was to work with artists to produce TFMCs designed to enhance environmental awareness. This objective was achieved through various workshops designed by the Food and Agriculture Organization of the United Nations (FAO, 1996). This was meant to guide artists in incorporating environmental messages into their work, to then be delivered in a performance.

The last objective was to study TFMCs to determine if they could be applied effectively in fostering environmental awareness among the people of the Tswaing region. An evaluation was initiated to determine if TFMCs effectively conveyed environmental messages to the audience. The audiences were observed to determine their reactions and to assess the effectiveness of the performance. Focus groups, informal interviews, descriptive field notes and video tapes allowed for proper analysis and interpretation of the situation.

Data analysis attempted to acquire an understanding of the study area's cultural context and how the communication systems operate within that area. This participatory project may not only promote TFMCs and their use in cultural and community development, but may also generate a methodology that could be useful for cultural research and training. Additionally, this project set out to demonstrate the relationship of culture and ecotourism.

Research Findings

For ecotourism to be promoted at Tswaing, both for educational and for local benefits, the inclusion of stories and narratives is necessary to develop appropriate programs. Ecotourism programmes should also consider the cultural context as it can be of great benefit to communities if properly incorporated into decision-making. Therefore, what follows are examples of stories and narratives which could be effectively applied to guide ecotourism planning.

Considering the cultural context

The success of this research depended in part on a basic understanding of the culture and communication channels of the area. While the natural environment has always been considered the focus in defining ecotourism, understanding the cultural context is essential in order to incorporate the beliefs of the area. It is important to highlight the interconnections between the natural, cultural and human environment. Having an awareness of the people's belief systems and practices is integral if authentic ecotourism is to be promoted within Tswaing.

Methods of communication such as songs, poems, dance and story-telling are deeply rooted in their cultural activities. These cultural activities include the importance of the marula tree, the *legotha* procedures, the chief's meetings and, most importantly, the link between modern beings and their ancestors. All stories come from the local cultures.

The communication process with the ancestors

Tswaing people communicate with the ancestors because they believe their spirits accompany them through life. Furthermore, this belief and subsequent communication demonstrates respect for those who have lived before them. The main contact with the ancestors is to solve problems, such as when a person does not have or is struggling for a job, when there is a problem with a marriage or even when a person encounters bad luck. An elder is usually asked to intercede and communicate with the ancestors on the petitioner's behalf.

Communication with the ancestors entails an entire process. First, the whole family gathers at the *Thokola* (a Pedi name meaning "meeting place"), where there are rocks and a marula tree. They sing and dance throughout the process. The family gathers around this specific private sacred place to discuss problems with their ancestors. When the family arrives at the *Thokola,* they place mixed herbs on the ground to welcome the ancestors. They bring with them an animal, usually a goat, but a chicken or cow may be used, depending on the seriousness of the problem. The animal must be a specific colour. In the Pedi culture, the goat must be brownish with a white neck. The goat is slaughtered as a sacrifice, and its blood must infiltrate the chosen area. They clean the blood until it disappears, butcher the animal and collect and bury all the bones. The last step of the communication process for awakening and speaking to the ancestors is to drink unfiltered malt beer, a traditional beer produced from fruit of the marula tree. They take a sip of the traditional malt beer and spit it on the ground and on one another. After all these procedures, the family can finally talk to the ancestors. They begin by talking to the first ancestor, then the second and the third, until they reach the last one who has died. They believe that by speaking to the ancestors their problems will be solved. This whole process is usually done early in the morning (5:00 a.m.) because discussing problems is a private affair.

The communication processes with the marula tree

The marula tree has great significance for the communication channels in the area. It is believed that the marula tree is a place of holiness, a place for meeting the ancestors referred to as *Gonzelo* in Tsonga, or a meeting place known as *Badimo* in Tswana and *Legotha* in Northern Sotho. The tree is not only a symbol used for calling the ancestors, but also for specific meetings such as religious gatherings, conferences, classroom discussion and meetings with the chiefs or the headman.

The communication process with the chief or the headman

According to the Tswana people, the communication process with the chief and the headman is of extreme importance. The marula tree is significant for the chiefs because they usually recite a traditional poem, only known by the men, to call for the rain. The tribal authorities walk to the nearby forest before sunrise and find people waiting for them. They sing, dance and play drums until the meeting takes place. The beat of the drums usually calls for the formation of clouds and for the rain to come. This symbol of calling for the rain is used during the plowing seasons, where only the chief of the community is allowed to plant the mealie (major staple of the area, also called maize). Once the chief plants the mealie, he must go to the marula tree to thank the ancestors for the rain.

The chief is responsible for solving problems in the village. The headman, however, is the mediator. A person with a problem goes to the headman who later goes to the chief for decisions. The chief always has the final say and, it is said, he usually makes his decisions with the help of the marula tree.

The communication process with the graveyards

Another of the region's significant rituals occurs at the graveyard near the crater. Out of respect for their ancestors, some people will cut a tree and let it fall on the deceased's grave. They will then drag the tree all the way to their homes, so the spirit of the ancestors is with them always.

The wiping wattle is another significant tree for some people, especially the Tsonga. When someone dies, they take the leaves of the tree and put them in water. They crush these leaves and the solution is sprayed on the body to chase evil spirits away and to welcome their new ancestors.

It is clear from these stories that the participants attach great importance to the communication process with their ancestors. Much of the symbolic interaction found in these cultural practices is found in the stories which accompany and give expression to them. A participatory map was created in this research to find more precise stories associated with Tswaing. Some of the stories, myths and legends provide significant environmental conservation principles and are detailed below.

The giant snake story

Within the region it is believed a giant snake lives at the crater. This snake, known as *Kokwana,* is obviously of great importance to the people, as most activities revolve around the story. Some claim to have seen it, others claim there is a cave full of bones in the north side of the crater, while others do not believe the legend at all. The significance behind the story has three distinct aspects: to keep people away during certain times of the day for preservation and conservation of the crater; to prevent people from coming to the crater so that animals have a place to drink; and the snake is believed to bring *sangomas* (traditional healers) to a secret place to train them. Because of these three distinct functions of the snake, some people show respect to the crater. It is believed that the snake has powers to preserve the crater and to teach *sangomas.*

The old man's story

Within the rural areas of Winterveld, an old man was a student of the giant snake before becoming a *sangoma.* Some people asserted that this old man stayed in training with the snake for six months. The old man lived at the crater on top of a rock located above a tree. On that rock there is a hollow place where he would collect water and share it with other animals. The old man always received a cooked meal and no one knows where those meals came from.

After the training of the old man was complete, the beat of drums called the old man to the village. He was wearing ornamental beads and bones as he was directed to the *Mashaba* (in Tswana, a place in the village to demonstrate that he was a real *sangoma*). The old man became "snake proof" as he would walk through the surrounding villages with many snakes wrapped around his body. They regarded the old man as a hero and an expert because the giant snake at the crater trained him. The old man died in 1993 with his story still remaining in the heart of many local people.

The sangomas (traditional healers)

The third item of cultural importance is the story of the *sangomas* within the region. Ordinary people with nightmares are believed to turn into *sangomas*. They go to a dream interpreter and are informed that they are ready to become *sangomas*. It is believed that the giant snake and other *sangomas* train the person who is having nightmares. The snake brings the *sangoma* into his or her home down in the lake, or to the north side of the crater where the snake trains a person to become a traditional healer. This training is a long process. After the training, the chief of the community will ask the *sangoma* to get something for him. The *sangoma* has to know where and what to find for the chief that is of healing significance. It is an initiation test to see if the snake or other *sangomas* trained the new *sangoma* properly.

The salt story

The crater is significant for ritualistic and religious activities because it produces salt. Some people believe a falling star created the crater, a miracle from God, providing them with salt minerals. To some, especially the Tswana and the Tsonga, the salt is extremely sacred. Some put salt in their yards and on their roofs to chase away evil spirits. They cover themselves with salt as protection from disease and bad luck because they believe the mineral has miraculous powers. According to the Tswana, the salt is also used to enable children to sleep safely. Others, especially the Zionist Christian Church and the Apostolic Church, collect the crater's water for ceremonial purposes.

Religious ceremonies at Tswaing

Apostolic Church members go to the crater every Thursday and Friday evening and spend the night at the crater. They remove their shoes and any jewellery containing metal and walk down to the crater lake with lit candles. Once at the bottom, they pray, dance and talk about particular problems that need to be solved. They believe in priests, not *sangomas*.

Zionist Christian Church members also pray at the site, at the highest point of the crater. They collect fresh water from the crater and pray all night.

Artists' respect for Tswaing

Below is a collection of songs, poems, and thoughts from the participants illustrating what Tswaing means to them in relation to the environment. A translation is provided.

A song:

"Sechaba Se Lebosa"	"The Nation Appreciated"
A re lebogeng	Let us appreciate
Slhaba sa Afrika	The African Nation
Re lebogela Maungo-Meriti le tsotlhe	We thank for the fruits-shelter and others
A re lebogeng	Let us appreciate
Slhaba sa Afrika	The African Nation
Re Lebogela metsi a btshelo	We thank you for the water and fire
A re logogeleng tlhago	Let us thank for the environment
A re rateng tlhaga	Let us love nature
A re tlhokomeleng tlhago	Let us conserve nature
A re agengtlhago	Let us build our environment
Re rata tlhago	We love nature

Amos Sachane (Tswana)

This song was collected from a young man who was wandering through Tswaing. When he was asked how important Tswaing was to him, he started singing this song. Surprisingly, others joined him and all the participants clearly knew the lyrics.

A story: **News by S.S. Twala** (a young sangoma in training at Tswaing, Tswana)

"We the herbal doctors, we love to live and live to the fullest with people. We help/heal people that are weak with things from the soil (ditswa mmling) meaning all the diseases. We dig natural herbs from the bush. We visit and check the bushes from near to far away to have a look of what types of herbs are there. The herbs are not the same, ie: others are from the roots while others are from the trunk to the leaves. The same as Tswaing it is a site of 2000 hectares with more than 400 species of flora. Tswaing protects life of people. You can find herbs, cattle, goats, birds and different type of reptiles."

The participants are not only committed to preserving and conserving the flora and fauna, but also to sharing dialogue about Tswaing. After the participatory mapping of those cultural features and personal interviews, it was evident that this area is strong in traditional culture. The participants placed great importance on the environmental and cultural activities at Tswaing, as is evident in the story about the snake and the *sangomas*. In that story, the participants identified environmental issues such as the conservation and preservation of herbs around the crater for the *sangomas* of the region. The *sangomas* play a significant role in people's lives; the people understand it is critical to preserve the Tswaing area and the medicinal herbs the *sangomas* need.

CULTURAL BELIEFS AND THE ENVIRONMENTAL CONTEXT FOR ECOTOURISM IN TSWAING

As seen above, stories, narratives, myths and legends associated with Tswaing are of extreme importance to the participants. Ecotourism practices should take such stories into consideration, as they are embedded in people's cultures.

Cultural beliefs are deeply rooted in the connection between people and their environment. Many songs, poems and recitals illustrate the significance placed on preservation, conservation and respect for the environment. Rapid population growth in the area presents a threat to Tswaing's natural environment. Tswaing is an unusual site and should receive significant conservation priorities because of its unique flora and fauna.

In this study, there are two interrelated views of nature conservation. First, nature conservation is seen as the preservation of certain natural areas by freeing them from human presence. This concept finds its origin in the legend of the giant snake living at the crater, a myth which serves to prevent people from disturbing the crater during certain hours, in order to preserve the area and permit animals to drink at the crater.

The other concept of nature conservation is based on the presence of humans in nature, rather than the need to separate humans from nature. This approach focuses on the responsibility of using natural resources while protecting their value for future generations. We could look at this concept with regard to the importance of *sangomas* in the region. The high respect for the *sangomas* at the crater is crucial to the region's conservation practices, because people know the *sangomas* need the fauna and flora in Tswaing.

Tswaing may, in fact, incorporate existing beliefs in its future environmental programmes and ecotourism activities. Such programmes are likely to educate people on the historical significance of the salt resources in Tswaing. Educational programmes could also examine Tswaing's flora and some of its medicinal purposes. The analogy of the giant snake could be an integral part of such programmes in the preservation and conservation of the Tswaing area. Programmes could also be developed around the marula tree, as it could effectively be used as a meeting place for tourists and school groups.

AN INVESTIGATION OF TRADITIONAL FOLK METHODS OF COMMUNICATION FOR ENVIRONMENTAL AWARENESS IN TSWAING

This study was intended not only to investigate and interpret the cultural context of Tswaing and its surrounding region, but also to work with local artists who produce songs, dances and poems associated with environmental issues. It investigated existing forms of communication and how they may contribute to environmental education.

Artists for this study were chosen based on specific criteria: their popularity, their involvement in Tswaing cultural activities, their ability to produce folk forms necessary for Tswaing's needs and their representation in the communities.

An inventory of each artist's form was essential to determine their potential contribution to environmental education. Each form was carefully examined and classified according to various criteria. Ranganath (1980a, 1980b) suggests the main criteria for classifying traditional folk methods of communication (TFMC): thematic content, cultural context, flexibility and form. Developing knowledge of each TFMC through an inventory allowed potential contributions to be determined. The artistic presentation was also classified according to the:

‣ other name(s) by which the form is known
‣ main messages of themes
‣ cultural symbols
‣ function
‣ purpose
‣ frequency
‣ venues
‣ occasion
‣ audiences reached
‣ audience participation
‣ availability of scripts
‣ language used

Consideration of this criteria was essential for understanding each TFMC and building in-depth knowledge of their functions, roles and capacities. A degree of familiarity with the TFMC was needed before undertaking any kind of communication project with the folk artists. It was critical to record the characteristics of the forms, and classify them into a "book of basic data", according to Ranganath (*ibid.*), in order to identify those with credible potential for communicating environmental awareness messages. A few significant artists were identified who have shown commitment to contribute to environmental education appropriate for Tswaing. The National Cultural History Museum (NCHM) could engage these artists to present ecotourism principles to the surrounding population and visitors. They are as follows:

Omm Diek Motan is a storyteller of the region who bases his thematic content on cultural and historical issues concerning Tswaing. He once worked in the salt factory and his main concern is to educate others about the history and cultural significance of the area. His aim is to alter people's perspectives on the Tswaing conservation area by providing evidence of past environmental problems. He tells stories all the time, going from house to house and school to school to deliver them. His audience is usually young children as he believes they are the ones who will make a difference in the future. He performs in English and in local African languages. Although his thematic content focuses on environmental awareness, his form does not seem very flexible because his messages illustrate the historical evolution of the Tswaing area. It therefore appeared difficult for incorporating new messages. His scripts are not available for future reference.

The Kromkuil Dance Group, also known as the Sivukile Cultural Group, examines social and cultural issues as they teach school children about different cultures. They also convey messages about peace and harmony. Their main concern is to educate and raise awareness pertaining to cultural identity and social issues. They perform once a month, mostly in primary and high schools where their audiences are predominantly female. They try to incorporate their audience into the performance. They perform in Zulu. The Kromkuil Dance Group's form is semi-flexible as they focus on maintaining and strengthening culture. Their popularity would enable them to reach many people. Incorporating new messages into their form is possible because the group is committed to raising environmental awareness.

The Dan Mashele Dance Group, also known as Natsanats, utilizes traditional singing and dancing to educate youth about violence. Dan Mashele, a former police officer, gets children off the streets and teaches them to dance to convey messages about stopping violence and crime in South Africa. They also sing and dance to raise funds to provide breakfast for street kids in the area. They are Tsonga and wear traditional dress with white body paint. Their objective is to change values in order to reduce crime and encourage people to report violent incidents to the police. They perform an average of twice a month at local schools, churches, market squares, and in Johannesburg. Due to their popularity, the Dan Mashele Dance group reaches a large audience each time they perform. Although the messages may reach all kinds of people, Mashele incorporates mostly elementary and high school children into the performances. The communication form is effective because its flexibility allows for the incorporation of new themes. Because the audience is involved in the performance, the communication potential is immense. Mashele believes that by highlighting social issues, the environment will also improve because people will become more aware of their surroundings. He also believes in teaching life skills to very young children, ages 4 to 14, so they will become good citizens and live in harmony with their environment. He performs in Tsonga and his scripts are available.

Jan Maja, a cartoonist, focuses solely on environmental issues in his drawings. He concentrates on the preservation and conservation of Tswaing. His main concern is to raise awareness and educate others about environmental concerns. He attempts to change people's values and attitudes toward their environment, as well as provide information. Out of his home, he draws a set of cartoons twice a month for the Tswaing Newsletter. As Maja personally distributes the newsletters, he reaches all the surrounding communities of Tswaing. His scripts are available to the NCHM as he writes in English and in Setswana. A talented artist, Maja makes significant contributions toward raising environmental awareness. He was identified for this project because his thematic content already incorporates environmental education; he uses his drawings to teach people not to litter or burn forests because these practices disturb the habitat and the environment at large. His drawings serve to educate others about taking care of their environment.

Mr. Nyamakazi, a *sangoma* also known as Ngaka and Isangoma, concentrates primarily on health and environmental issues. His main theme is preserving the environment so that he can retrieve herbs, roots, leaves and other medicinal plants for his practice. His main concerns are to teach others and raise awareness of traditional medicine. He does this by wearing the traditional *sangoma* costume. From his office in Winterveld, he makes himself available to provide health information and he performs monthly or as requested. He reaches people of both genders from age 35 to 45, most of whom have never been to school. His scripts are not available as he relies mostly on his ancestors. He performs in Zulu, Tsonga, and Northern Sotho. He is an advisory councillor and the chairperson of *sangomas* in the region. His form proved to be semi-flexible because of his focus on traditional medicine and the communication process through the ancestors. Therefore, it may prove difficult to incorporate new messages into his form. However, Mr. Nyamakazi contributes greatly in environmental education and health awareness because he has a direct relationship with the environment for medicinal purposes. His main concern is to inform people about how to live compatibly with the environment and how to use the environment in a sustainable manner.

The Pedi Traditional Dance Group, also known as Leboya, teaches people about their culture and way of life. They perform four times a month in their communities and around the country. The audience they reach are mostly females, who are incorporated into their performances. They perform in Northern Sotho. Their communication potential may prove semi-flexible because their main interest is teaching others about their own culture. Unfortunately, because they are a group of 17 elder women with strong cultural values, incorporating a new message could prove difficult. The Pedi Traditional Dance Group relies on cultural symbols reflected in their costumes, with blue, green, and yellow representing sky, trees, and sun. This could prove to be an important tool for conveying messages. Their costumes use recycled materials which could be represented in environmental programs.

Richard Matlhabe, a poet, makes a great contribution by informing others about the preservation and conservation of Tswaing. As well as writing about Tswaing, he brings people to the area to teach them about its cultural and natural significance. He informs people about specific trees and tells stories about animals living in the area. His communication potential could prove significant as he has never performed before, which makes it easier to incorporate a new message into his work. His poems could contribute significantly toward raising awareness about the Tswaing conservation area.

All the artists have their own talented works and functions that affect their communities. They can each make a significant contribution in their own distinct way of conveying messages. Most groups focus on social issues such as violence, but some had the advantage of already having environmental education themes in their work.

What follows is an interpretation of how the process was intiated with each group to incorporate new messages into their work, as well as a description of the results as observed during the actual performances.

FROM PROCESS TO A PERFORMANCE

Workshops with local artists were developed to link culture to the environment and ecotourism. During communication workshops, strategies for incorporating new messages concerning environmental awareness were developed. A number of participatory exercises helped participants to identify the most important environmental issues in their areas. Brainstorming and ranking of important environmental issues was undertaken with the participants. As the work progressed, the participants tied cultural significance to environmental issues. For example, they identified the significance of the Tswaing wetlands as the source of grass used to make baskets, the importance of Tswaing herbs for *sangomas* and the importance of the salt for ritual and religious purposes. During the workshops, the words culture and environment could not be separated. The workshop participants became committed to working with what the communities valued. They struggled to incorporate the new themes into their productions while not altering their usual performance. This suggests that for existing programs, incorporating local beliefs, values and practices is essential.

Songs, dances and poems were generated as the workshops progressed. What was produced did not necessarily focus on environmental problems specific to their areas, but on nature conservation in general. Most participants believed in the link between their culture and the environment. In examining why the participants generated TFMCs geared toward environmental preservation and conservation, they realized those themes were in harmony with the cultural beliefs of the participants.

A performance entitled "Environmental and Cultural Awareness" was held at Tswaing on December 16, 1997. More than a thousand people attended. The excellent attendance indicates that TFMC is valued, accepted and may prove to be a source of inspiration for the rural population. TFMC is not only an entertainment tool used to inform others, but is also a two-way communication, ideal for generating new thoughts and ideas about subjects such as these.

The groups who performed presented environment education themes, focusing on how conservation affects their lives.

The Kromkuil Dance Group conveyed a message about preserving their livestock because of its importance in the marriage ritual.

The Pedi Traditional Dance Group's message was about becoming self-sufficient and strengthening their culture by connecting their environment with their work. They showed that they recycle material for their clothing and use material from nature for subsistence. The colours of their traditional costumes represent nature. They wear blue as a symbol of the sky to call rain, yellow as a symbol of the sun and green to represent the forest. They believe that trees offer a great deal for medicinal purposes and food. Through the many symbols reflected in their clothing, the Pedi Traditional Dance Group conveys messages about the way they live and what the environment has to offer their lifestyle. Most people's responses to performance was to say they had learned about their natural environment.

The Dan Mashele Dance Group conveyed their environmental messages through singing, drumming and traditional costume, which kept the audience interested. They involved the audience by asking what the environment meant to them. The audience would call out answers like "Yes, we love our environment" and "No, we will not abuse our environment anymore". Mashele left time for people to reflect and to ask for further information after the performance.

CONCLUSION: A HOLISTIC APPROACH TO THE ENVIRONMENT FOR ECOTOURISM PURPOSES

This study suggests that environment and culture are fundamentally linked and this linkage needs to be brought out in ecotourism activities. Many people's reliance on the past, and a circular approach of connecting environment and culture points to a holistic framework for ecotourism purposes. The natural and cultural contexts can not be divorced. Environmental principles are deeply rooted in the beliefs of the cultures in the study area. The importance of the past and ancestors, environmental symbols such as the marula tree, the *sangomas,* calling the rain and the function of salt in ritual are significant in most people's lives.

The communication processes presented by the artists had a direct connection with the cultural beliefs of the area. The performances were based on themes of cultural and environmental awareness, and the groups connected environmental issues with daily life and cultural practice.

The importance of incorporating culture into environmental education is self-evident. One of the major lessons learned was that people utilize culture to learn new concepts. Moreover, they adapt to new ideas that can be rooted in their own culture and expressed through dance and song. It is necessary to acknowledge the stories that help people make sense of their lives in relation to the Tswaing crater. The performances were much more effective than simply communicating precautions against littering. To the people of Tswaing, the word environment is related to cultural beliefs and their fundamental existence. The environmental principles attached to these beliefs are embedded deeply in the social and cultural matrix of this area.

For ecotourism purposes, facilitating the learning process is of critical importance. Ecotourism activities were used as an educational experience for both the visitors and the local people. Working with existing cultural communication channels proved critical to deliver messages related to environmental education. It is not prudent to impose new methods of communication, but instead to work with what is already familiar and recognizable for delivering new ideas. This research shows that if concepts are presented in terms familiar to the community, they are more likely to be accepted and have greater impact. The artists had the talent to convey the messages and the public responded to this form of communication because they were able to identify with the artists.

REFERENCES

Ascroft, J. and Masilele, S. 1989: From Top-down to Co-equal Communication: Popular Participation in Development Decision-making. Paper presented at the seminar on *Participation: A Key Concept in Communication and Change.* Pune: University of Poona.

Coller, Van H., Damaneyt, A., De Jong, R., Kussel, U. and Reimold, W. 1995: *Tswaing Museum Research Project.* Unpublished report. Pretoria: National Cultural History Museum.

Damaneyt, A. 1995: A People's Museum: Tswaing Case Study. *Samab,* 22 (2), 13-14.

De Jong, R. 1996: *The Tswaing Crater Museum.* Unpublished report. Pretoria: National Cultural History Museum.

De Jong, R. 1997: *A Short History of the Settlements around Tswaing.* Unpublished report. Pretoria: National Cultural History Museum.

De Jong, R. and Reimold, W. 1995: The Tswaing Crater Museum; Rediscovery 200 Millennia of History. *African Panorama,* 40 (3), 34-35.

Food and Agriculture Organization. 1996: *Artists as Experts: a Participatory Methodology to Produce Traditional and Popular Media, Based on a Population Communication in Africa.* Rome: Food and Agriculture Organization of the United Nations, Development Support Branch.

Hatting, P.S. and Moolman, H.N. 1996: *The Tswaing Crater Museum: Addressing Institutional, Community and Environmental Needs.* Unpublished report. Pretoria: University of Pretoria and National Cultural History Museum.

Jones, Alison. 1995: *Dictionary of World Folklore.* New York: Larouse.

Kidd, R. 1982: *The Popular Performing Arts, Non-formal Education and Social Change in the Third World: a bibliography and review essay.* The Hague: Center for the Study of Education in Developing Countries (CESO).

Kidd, R. and Colletta, N. 1980: *Tradition for Indigenous Structures and Folk Media in Non-Formal Education.* Berlin: German Foundation for International Development and International Council for Adult Education.

Kussel, U.S. 1996a: People Participate to Create a Sustainable Environment. The Tswaing Crater Museum, a Case Study. *Focus,* 8-11.

Kussel, U.S. 1996b: *What Does it Mean to Me: Workshop on Public Participation in Development and the Environment.* Unpublished report. Delta Environmental Center.

Madu, M. 1986: Folk Media and Communication. *Man-and-Development,* 8 (3), 151-168.

Ranganath, H.K. 1980a: *Folk Media and Communication.* Bangalore: Chinthana Prakashana.

Ranganath, H.K. 1980b: *Using Folk Entertainment to Promote National Development.* Population Communication Manuals. Paris: UNESCO.

UNESCO. 1982: Recommendations of Experts Meeting on the Integrated Use of Folk Media and Mass Media in Support of Population/Family Planning Programme. *Folk Media and Mass Media in Population Communication.* Paris: UNESCO.

Chapter 9

The Clanwilliam Living Landscape Project

by John Parkington, Sandra Prosalendis, Alicia Monis, Rushdi Nackerdien, Juanita Pastor, Colette Peitersen, Nina Cohen, Hilton Judin, Jenny Sandler and Mary Leslie

The Living Landscape Concept

Living landscape is a community-based museum and schools curriculum project located in the small, rural Western Cape town of Clanwilliam, South Africa. Founded in 1812, and originally known as Jan Dissels Vallei, Clanwilliam was for much of the 19th century a frontier settlement, in which the politics of colonialism were played out against the magnificent backdrop of the Cederberg mountains. Now, in another era of political reorganisation, the current citizens are attempting to construct a democratic future and put aside a divided past. As in most rural Cape towns, the divisions take the form of white town, coloured township and black informal settlement. Our project seeks to support these attempts at reconciliation by revealing and celebrating the history of those who were previously denied a contribution

The objective of living landscape is to use the local landscape as a framework for integrating the learning process and for reconnecting particularly the descendants of indigenous people with a past from which they were largely severed by colonialism. It is thus a programme that seeks to empower people by establishing an accessible archive of historical, archaeological and environmental information with explicit links to a new schools curriculum and new heritage legislation.

By creating a sense of local ownership over this heritage landscape, local people will be enabled and encouraged to look after its particular cultural qualities, monitor damage, and participate effectively in creating a tangible sense of custodianship. In this way, future damage, disrepair or simply neglect of their heritage, can be minimized.

Furthermore, the living landscape concept provides an opportunity for local people to take an active interest in the evolution of various possible future landscapes for the Clanwilliam area. The current interest in community involvement that is characteristic of environmental management and development programmes in South Africa is a very real issue for the furtherance of this project. This proposal provides a framework to link social and environmental programmes to the process of creating futures that create wealth, expand employment and sustain the environment.

We argue here that the creation of a landscape-oriented educational effort will lead to better articulated and more effective community involvement in sustainable development for the region. Empowerment means granting people self-respect through the processes of education, building confidence and trust. Education through active engagement in past and future landscape change is a valuable tool in the empowerment process.

This project, therefore, provides an opportunity to relate history to futurity via empowerment, education and the building of training schemes for landscape interpretation and environmental evaluation. These tools are vital for long-term land use and natural resource management in South Africa as a whole. They also provide a basis for extending the value added by tourism to the poor rural areas, where meaningful interpretative capacities are currently underdeveloped. Over the next few years, we plan to build a series of structures in chosen localities in the landscape that will act as learning places, resource centres and research opportunities for rural, previously disadvantaged, people.

THE CLANWILLIAM LANDSCAPE

The Clanwilliam landscape is richly endowed with remains of past social and natural histories. In geological terms, the landscape reflects the momentous events of glacial action, dramatic mountain building and the fossil record of previous life forms. In archaeological terms, there are many thousands of rock paintings and rock shelter sites left by hunter-gatherers and herders whose culture was all but extinguished by the colonial presence. In historical terms, there are buildings and other residues of farming and agriculture that document a rapidly changing social landscape. On the maps there are tantalizing traces, in the form of indigenous place names, of the precolonial landscape and its places. In botanical and zoological terms, Clanwilliam is home to the Fynbos Biome, one of the world's six plant kingdoms, and the smallest of them. The plants and animals are themselves a residue of past living communities that once included elephants, rhino and lion, some of them painted on cave walls.

We see the fossils, the rock art, the place names, the plant and animal communities, the rock record and the ruined buildings as traces of the past, reflections of what was, and practical opportunities to re-learn, re-claim and re-habilitate. Histories have been denied, languages have been lost and cultural identities have been denigrated as people, too, became traces in a changing social landscape. The re-claiming and re-connecting can form the basis of an integrated school curriculum where the results of research into local history, archaeology, architecture, botany, zoology, geology and palaeontology form a resource archive.

We will use the environmental context to develop a unique architectural proposal, in which a network of structures relocates in the landscape. In placing the exhibit back at the point of discovery at the actual site of rock paintings, fossil remains and vegetation, a number of dialogues are encouraged. If objects are not removed from sites in which they are found but rather contextualized in place, then their display can be set off against their original condition. The immediate presentation is contrasted with a deep geographical and historical past. This potential for re-discovery is a continuous dialogue between natural and artificial, containment and release, near and far, then and now.

Each locality will be opened with an exhibition and each display will include a text on the topic covered. The objective is to accumulate information on the traces that exist in the landscape, so that teachers will have a growing set of teaching materials, classroom ideas and actual specimens for their use. The active involvement of students and faculty from a wide range of departments at University of Cape Town (UCT) will offer practical opportunities for school pupils to get involved in the gathering of knowledge as envisaged in the new curriculum 2005 document. It is also envisaged that archaeological records of the local heritage sites will be transferred back to Clanwilliam and that pupils will be able to actively research and help conserve their local heritage, as envisaged in upcoming heritage legislation.

Figure 9.1 Location of exhibition and teaching structures on the Clanwilliam landscape

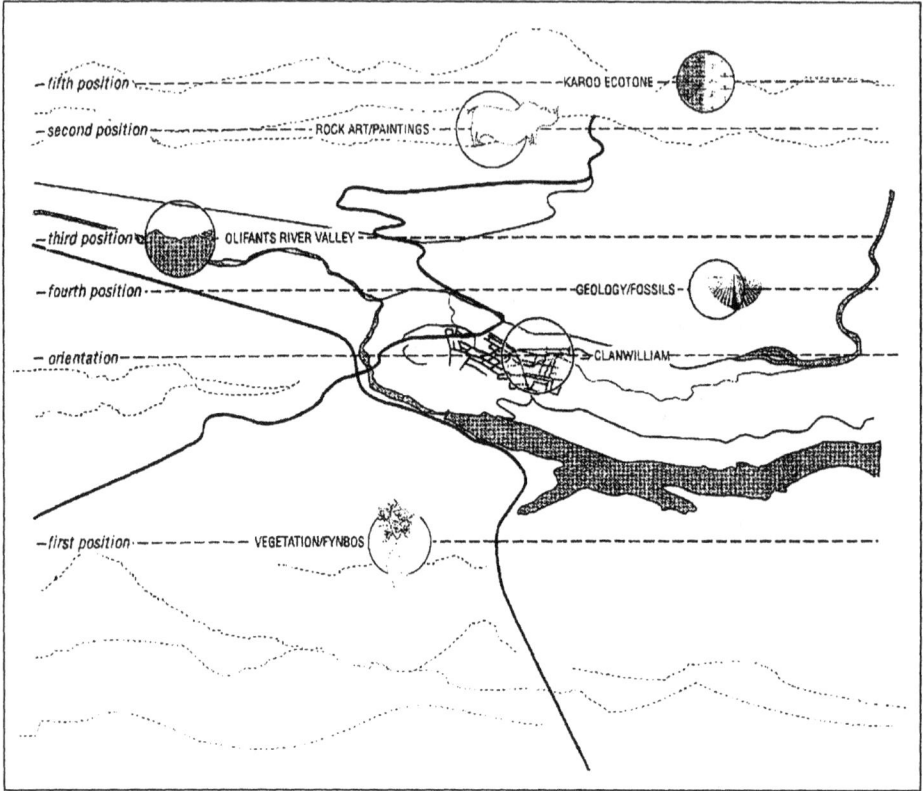

- fifth position —— ——— KAROO ECOTONE ———
- second position —— —— ROCK ART/PAINTINGS ——
- third position —— OLIFANTS RIVER VALLEY ——
- fourth position —— ——— GEOLOGY/FOSSILS ——
- orientation —— CLANWILLIAM ——
- first position —— VEGETATION/FYNBOS ——

Figure 9.1 shows the location of the exhibition and teaching structures on the Clanwilliam landscape. Each position is chosen to illustrate and explain a particular component of the living landscape: rock art; fossils; fynbos ecology; landscape structure. The buildings will be designed to fit the exhibits.

Living landscape will establish a radically new kind of museum in which display cases and exhibition rooms are dispersed back into the landscape from which the objects and information came. The localities will each focus on one particular component of the landscape trace – rock art in a cave setting, fossil animals in a rock section, a fynbos plant community, a viewing point to understand the valley structure – and will be used as extramural classrooms for scholars and other groups. In Clanwilliam itself, we will develop an orientation locale in which records of research of all kinds will be concentrated, and in which computers will provide global access to electronic resources for young people. Notice boards at all schools in the town will signpost and advertise the availability of resources at the other localities.

The whole museum, therefore, is completely decentralized and located with respect to the landscape at archaeological and other strategic positions: *a first position* for the display, dissection and illustration of fynbos vegetation; *a second position* for the identification of rock paintings with accompanying descriptive tracings and explanations; *a third position* as a lookout onto the Olifants River valley with mapping devices; *a fourth position* for fossils in a trench that descends in layers exhibiting the findings in context; *a fifth position* at the edge of the Karoo ecotone with an exploration of the plant, animal and soil surrounding framework; *a series of initiating positions* as information boards at each school; and *an orientation position* as an administrative and meeting area in Clanwilliam.

The Krakadouw Centre

In the town of Clanwilliam, we propose to establish a research and resource centre which will form the focus of a University of Cape Town outreach programme, with participation from many UCT departments. We have held a number of open meetings in Clanwilliam with a representative series of interest groups, all of which have clearly pointed to the need to address the question of how the past is represented and by whom. The Clanwilliam Museum is currently housed in the Gaol and depicts the activities of the advantaged white community. There is an urgent need to redress this imbalance and collect histories that allow all citizens to find themselves and celebrate their past. We hope to do this alongside the establishment of a centre that situates history in its landscape context.

This centre, which we tentatively call the Krakadouw Centre, will house records, maps and objects that have resulted from many years of research by a wide range of people from archaeology to zoology. The proposal is to relocate the evidence to Clanwilliam and to use it as a contribution to the revised school syllabus, which calls for localization, integration and restructuring of teaching in a research rather than a rote learning mode. It is our intention to mount regular exhibitions of accumulated knowledge of the Clanwilliam region and its social and natural history, meshing science with humanity into one integrated study.

Our vision is of an archive which would include visual, artefactual and electronic resources that will be accessed by both pupil and teacher, regularly supported and supplied by visits from interested researchers from Cape Town. The orientation hub would thus act as a laboratory for teaching a range of practical skills, including numeracy, computer literacy, map-reading, conservation awareness, resource management, survey and the collection of social and environmental information.

Funding is now being sought for some renovation to St. Johns School in Clanwilliam which will become the Krakadouw Centre. This small primary school has enormous symbolic value for the coloured residents and represents all that is left of two schools and a church used by this community until sold and, partly, demolished some years ago. The buildings that stand include three classrooms, a school hall and a small cottage; these latter two are much older than the classrooms and were originally thatched. The hall will make an excellent exhibition and workshop space, the cottage can be turned easily into an office and computer centre and the classrooms will become accommodation for student and scholar groups.

RECLAIMING LANGUAGE, KNOWLEDGE AND HISTORY

It is a noticeable irony in Clanwilliam that most local people, with strong links to the indigenous pre-colonial population, never visit the museum, appear to have little interest in the local rock art, and have no control over local heritage sites. The colonial population spread rapidly through the northwestern Cape in the early 18th century and renamed the landscape as they appropriated the land, decimated the game and turned local hunters and herders (those they didn't slaughter) into farm labourers. As a result, almost all traces of the languages, ethno-science and cultural history of indigenous people were lost or treated as insignificant. Interestingly, there are many reminders of the pre-colonial landscape in the form of place names which still retain their indigenous reference. In this project, we map and document these traces and explore the gradual renaming of places by a succession of newcomers who recognized that to name was to claim. Several of the remaining indigenous names refer to passes or routes through the mountains, names such as Krqakadouw, Nardouw, Cardouw, Kriedouwkrans, or Gydo, all of which retain the root dao, or "path", from the original name. Others, such as Tarakamma or Matsikamma, retain the root *kamma* for "water", the former being reliably an aboriginal word for part of the Olifants River. Still others are more enigmatic, such as Koekenaap, Goerap or Hantam. Researching these names leads to the general issue of reclaiming indigenous languages, of which only Nama remains in the Western Cape.

Figure 9.2 Our lost languages

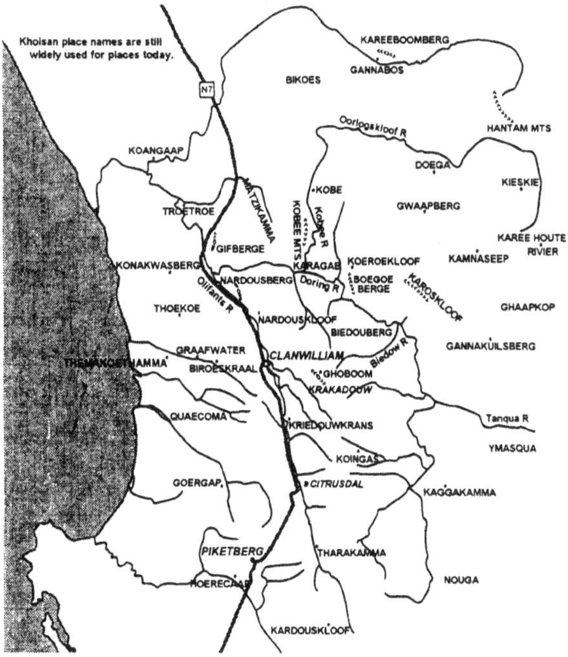

Many places are still known by their indigenous names (see Figure 9.2). We assembled these names and produced a map of the Clanwilliam landscape which has survived the extinction of indigenous languages. These names form the basis of a rediscovery of lost languages and became one of the themes of the Living Landscape exhibit opened on Heritage Day 1997 in the St. Johns School.

Apart from place names, the most frequent survivals of indigenous words seem to be in plant names, where *buchu* and *dacha* are fully integrated into other languages. But there are many more plants that still retain their indigenous names, such as *kambroo, gwhaap* or *canna,* many of them still collected by rural communities. The research on edible and medicinal plants allows us to remember the vast store of knowledge possessed by indigenous hunter-gatherers and herders, amounting to a deep understanding on their part of the active chemical ingredients of plants that had nutritional or medicinal value. There exists among the rural community of Clanwilliam an ideal opportunity to collect surviving traces of an ethno-botanical knowledge that extends back into prehistory, and is almost gone. Ironically, while this knowledge is downplayed or ignored in the local museum, international pharmaceutical companies are scouring the literature for hints as to marketable products in the local vegetation, and finding them. Given the prominence of the rooibos tea industry in the displays of the Clanwilliam Museum, this selective amnesia would be an excellent metaphor for the social injustice that needs to be addressed in the town.

During the colonial period, black and brown Clanwilliam people were written out of history, and this was reinforced by the imbalance in literate observers and published works. In the present displays in the Clanwilliam Museum, these groups are barely reflected, and then only in supportive or silent roles. We have already started to collect oral histories from local people whose ancestors have lived on the local farms or in Clanwilliam itself for many generations. Our intention is to exhibit materials that will both broaden and lengthen the notion of history presently used in the museum. People will talk and write themselves back into history.

ROCK ART IN THE LANDSCAPE

Over the past 25 years we have located, recorded and studied about 2,000 rock art sites in the western part of the Cape, many of them in the Clanwilliam landscape. These images, which probably number some tens of thousands in the vicinity of the town, are a complex reflection of the religious and symbolic lives of the artists. Far from a simple record of animals and social activities, the paintings were a marking of the landscape with signs and reminders of appropriate social behaviour. They tell not of what people do but of what people are. They remain today as a poignant reminder of a people culturally extinct. Unfortunately, the paintings are often defaced by people ignorant of their historical and symbolic value, who write their names over them or chip away at them. It is our responsibility to try to protect traces by education, surely the best fence we can put around them.

In this project we plan to return our records of these paintings to Clanwilliam in the form of tracings, maps and electronic site information so that the archive can become accessible to local people. In addition, we believe that local groups, including scholars, can develop a system of conservation by increasing local awareness of the beauty, fragility and vulnerability of the art. More than that, local people can act as monitors of damage by establishing a schedule of site visits that will detect damage and begin the process of reparation. What we envisage is a monitoring and conservation group, based in the local schools, which will assume responsibility for visiting and checking the status of rock painting sites as well as for supervising the removal of any graffiti that appear. This will eventually be offered to all local landowners as a service and will involve local people quite practically in the conservation. Unless we involve the local residents, we see little chance of protecting the many thousands of rock paintings of the region. The conservation awareness can be expanded to include the geological fossils and architectural traces that are as significant as the paintings in defining the local natural and cultural heritage.

Figure 9.3 Clapping Ladies rock painting

Figure 9.3 illustrates a tracing of a painting we call Clapping Ladies. Unfortunately, this painting is no longer visible. It has been destroyed by the raising of a dam wall and the flooding of the rock wall on which the image was made.

The model of placing the responsibility for conservation in local communities is not new and promises to generate not only renewed awareness in local achievements, but also jobs in a revived archaeo-tourism industry. The upcoming heritage legislation encourages non-governmental organizations concerned about heritage to get involved in identifying, proclaiming and preserving sites of communal significance. If the study and understanding of the paintings becomes part of the school curriculum, as it should, then a conservation ethic will become one outcome. Other likely outcomes will be the ability to read, interpret and make maps, and an understanding of the value of computer records as management tools.

The appropriate location for the tracings, slides and written records of the rock art sites is the Krakadouw Centre in Clanwilliam, where a curator can monitor the school use of them. We also plan to build one of the museum structures at a rock art site in the field where original painted images can be viewed and explained on site. Considerable research has been undertaken in South Africa and elsewhere on the potentials and risks in exposing rock paintings to regular viewing by groups of children or interested adults. We envisage more than simply a viewing platform, and plan to develop both a set of written texts that explain how to look at the paintings, how to decode them and thus gain a better understanding of their meaning, and also a visual key that will guide the eye to specific details and begin to build a frame of reference for future viewing.

We are also very much aware that structures which stand largely unattended in the veld must be secure and able to withstand both the natural elements and the attentions of an initially uninformed public. The structure envisaged will be a durable and flexible design which will unfold to provide vertical and horizontal surfaces. Vertical wooden screens become descriptive frameworks for maps, texts for demonstration, spatial diagrams that underpin explanations. Stone surfaces act as path and inscription. Wooden panels serve as working surfaces and stage. Elements are slid, opened, joined or unfolded as blackboards, backdrops, shelves, tables or tablets. After each visit they can be shut and enclosed for the next.

CLANWILLIAM LANDSCAPE: PAST AND PRESENT

Clanwilliam boasts a remarkably beautiful landscape. Scattered across the hills and fields are dramatic remnants of past life, survivals from earlier times and traces of events hard to imagine in the present landscape. It is our conviction that these fragments are the hooks upon which to hang a curriculum that will grab the attention of local children and make learning relevant and fun. Aided by the provision of internet facilities, teachers will be able to tap into a global encyclopaedia of knowledge to identify, explain and research a host of issues that are plainly visible in the landscape. We envisage pupils engaging in practical projects that take them out into the local veld and allow them to record, observe, manipulate and handle real research material. Some obvious opportunities are listed below.

Clanwilliam enjoys now a Mediterranean-type winter rainfall climate and lies in a stable mountainous valley, with abundant water provided by the Olifants River. But buried in the local rock sequence are fossils of animals that lived in glacial lakes; on the local hillsides are the marks caused by huge glaciers; and the mountains themselves are evidence of massive faulting, slumping and warping of rock strata. At one time, Clanwilliam Bay was a large embayment in an ancient sea located between the mountains now under the Atlantic Sea and those of the present Karoo region. As the nearby glaciers melted, the lakes housed hundreds of now extinct forms of life which are perfectly preserved in the clays of the Clanwilliam landscape. Many millions of years later, early people ranged along the banks of the Palaeo-Olifants River in search of giant zebras, giant buffalo, giant hartebeest and other animals now long extinct. These sites and the evidence they hold will fuel the interest and excitement of young people and lead them inevitably to the study of palaeontology, archaeology and geology.

The plant communities of the Clanwilliam landscape belong to the Fynbos Biome, one of the six plant kingdoms of the world, the most diverse but easily the smallest of them. Famous among botanists, it has a bewildering variety of species and associations, including the Clanwilliam cedar groves, which are probably a relic from times when conditions were both wetter and colder than now. In fact, the Fynbos is itself a phenomenon of persistent climatic and environmental change that saw communities repeatedly retreating to mountainous refuges as conditions became temporarily unsuitable. The Fynbos, with its particular set of animal and plant associations is on the doorstep of Clanwilliam pupils and provides a natural entry point for the study of botany, zoology and environmental science. It is not hard to picture scholars collecting rainfall information, measuring the flow of the Olifants River, counting animal tracks as a way to assess numbers, and helping on palaeontological and archaeological digs. Such involvement will engender a real and permanent sense of the value of conservation and the need for sustainable use of the local landscape. Workshops with teachers from all three Clanwilliam schools have convinced us that there is a great enthusiasm on their part to receive materials and implement new practices.

LANDSCAPE AWARENESS AND LEADERSHIP PROGRAMME

The landscape, with its varied traces of past forms of life, ancient artefacts and cultural remains, and rock and sediment history, is a natural laboratory in which to teach an integrated school curriculum. We propose here programmes for scholars and teachers, offering an introduction to both the natural and the historical sciences through exploring the landscape within a framework for learning and teaching. Three days of field sessions, supported by texts designed to expose and explain features of the natural and cultural landscape, are supervised by researchers and guides with experience in ecology, history, archaeology and architecture. The object is to develop a series of skills, including an ability to read maps; an understanding of environmental processes; an awareness of the need to conserve fragile biological and cultural resources; and an ability to read the traces on the landscape. We believe that the experiences of young people in exploring and understanding the landscape will be empowering and will help to generate leadership qualities in the participants.

The newly acquired UCT field station in the old St. Johns primary school in Clanwilliam is being renovated and expanded for use in a wide range of community-related projects and programmes. When completed, with the aid of university funding, there will be bunk accommodation for groups of up to 30 scholars or students. The object of this programme is to offer Western Cape schools a three-day package during which archaeological, historical, architectural, botanical, palaeontological and geological traces are visited and explained. A separate package for teachers is envisaged so that the lessons of environmental awareness, conservation and process can be strengthened and supported in prior and subsequent classroom exercises.

The framework of sites used will be a series of installations built on localities in the landscape chosen as places suitable as explanatory stations. Briefly, these stations will be equipped as temporary fold-out classrooms in which some specific trace on the landscape can be experienced and understood. The course will tour the stations and reinforce the lessons of the field with discussions and exhibits back at the hub in the St. Johns primary school in Clanwilliam. A group of interested academics from UCT have volunteered their services to provide literature and, in some cases, specimens for use in demonstrations and exercises.

We have already begun to copy material from a variety of geological, archaeological and ecological texts which need to be rewritten in a language suitable for young scholars. We plan to produce a textbook on Learning from the Landscape, which can be regularly updated and which will contain outlines of classroom activities and worksheets. Funding is needed to support the production of these texts and the structuring and workshopping of the idea behind the field course. It is our intention to use local people as guides wherever this is possible. The need here is to school such people in the concept of living landscape and to equip them to lead the field excursions and workshops. This is a form of empowerment and job-creation that is sorely needed in the rural, fairly impoverished environment of Clanwilliam. In addition, we seek some bursary support to offer to local schools in order to make their participation possible.

ACKNOWLEDGEMENTS

We want to thank our friends in Clanwilliam, who not only welcomed our initiative but were prepared to join us in forming a Clanwilliam Committee. In particular we are grateful to Willem Fransman, Doreen du Plessis, Magda Gordon, Flip Lochner, Evelyn Ferreira, Dennis Parring, Margaret Bergh and Marie Schreuder for many helpful meetings and discussions. Senile and Pieter Holloway were really hospitable focal points and Willem Fransman performed miracles with the St. Johns Hall. Tim O'Riordan gave us some extremely timely advice for which we thank him. Funding for the Living Landscape project has come from the ECEP programme, administered by the Universities of Guelph and Cape Town, and the Department of Arts, Culture, Science and Technology. To both of these organizations we owe a huge debt of thanks.

INDEX